Foreword

The F-16 was the first fighter capable of pulling 9G right off the runway. Its design is pleasing to the eye, its performance is eyewatering and its capabilities are truly multi-role, capable of performing every modern tactical combat mission. It's been in production for more than 50 years and has been involved in all the major conflicts of our time, including strikes on Iran under the Israeli-US Operation Epic Fury.

Designed by General Dynamics, the prototype YF-16, serial number 72-1567, was officially flown for the first time by the late test pilot Phil Oestricher at Edwards Air Force Base, California on February 2, 1974, although the aircraft had made an unscheduled flight at Edwards 14 days earlier on January 20.

The first production Block 1 F-16A for the US Air Force, serial number 78-0001, was delivered to Edwards on September 6, 1978. The USAF took delivery of 2,231 Fighting Falcons, the last of which – Block 50 F-16C, serial 01-7053 – was delivered to Shaw Air Force Base on March 25, 2005.

Thirty-one nations currently operate the F-16, with Argentina and Ukraine being the most recent nations to join the Viper club. The USAF has the largest fleet, with dozens of aircraft conducting peacetime deterrence missions in Europe and Southeast Asia, as well as combat operations in the Middle East.

Lockheed Martin has continued to improve the F-16 with development of the latest Block 70 version, integration of the APG-83 AESA radar, the Viper avionics upgrade, an air-to-ground strike missile dubbed the AGM-88J stand-in attack weapon, the AGR-20F fixed-wing, air-launched, counter-unmanned aircraft system (a rocket used to shoot down drones) and a self-protection system known as the ALQ-257 Integrated Viper Electronic Warfare System.

After a 50-plus year history, the F-16 remains the most prolific fighter aircraft of its generation, combat proven, affordable and still in the race for fighter aircraft competitions around the world. Despite Colombia's selection of the Saab JAS 39E Gripen rather than the F-16, Peru looks to be the next nation to join the Viper club.

Born and raised in Texas, the F-16 continues to flourish from Greenville, South Carolina.

Mark Ayton
Editor

US Air National Guard/MSgt George Perkins

CONTENTS

USAF/Senior Airman Nicholas Paczkowski

Fuerza Aérea Argentina

Ukrainian Air Force Command

USAF/Senior Airman Joshua Hoskins

ISBN: 978 1 83632 256 6
Editor: Mark Ayton
Senior editor, specials: Roger Mortimer
Email: roger.mortimer@keypublishing.com
Cover Design: Steve Donovan
Design: SJmagic DESIGN SERVICES, India
Advertising Sales Manager: Sam Clark
Email: sam.clark@keypublishing.com
Tel: 01780 755131
Advertising Production: Becky Antoniades
Email: Rebecca.antoniades@keypublishing.com

SUBSCRIPTION/MAIL ORDER
Key Publishing Ltd, PO Box 300, Stamford, Lincs, PE9 1NA
Tel: 01780 480404
Subscriptions email: subs@keypublishing.com
Mail Order email: orders@keypublishing.com
Website: www.keypublishing.com/shop

PUBLISHING
Group CEO: Adrian Cox
Publisher: Steve O'Hara

Published by
Key Publishing Ltd, PO Box 100, Stamford, Lincs, PE9 1XQ
Tel: 01780 755131
Website: www.keypublishing.com

PRINTING
Precision Colour Printing Ltd, Haldane, Halesfield 1, Telford, Shropshire. TF7 4QQ

DISTRIBUTION
Frontline Distribution Solutions Ltd, 2 Poultry Avenue, London, EC1A 9PU
Enquiries: 02074 294000 or info@flgroup.co.uk

Radars, Pods, Missiles and Munitions

Insight into many of the major systems and weapons employed by the F-16.

Northrop Grumman's CRJ flight testbed fitted with an F-16 nose radome housing an APG-83 radar unit. Northrop Grumman

The most valuable – and costly – element of future upgrades to F-16 fighters is an active electronically scanned array (AESA) radar. An AESA retrofit increases F-16 capability across multiple mission areas, especially air-to-air against low radar cross section targets such as stealth aircraft, cruise missiles and unmanned air vehicles.

In 2013, the SABR Block 1.0 was selected for the upgrade of Taiwan's Block 20 F-16A/F-16B fleet and the Block 2.0 version for USAF F-16Cs and F-16Ds. It was seen as a likely system for future US Foreign Military Sale (FMS) programmes and assured commonality with the Combat Avionics Programmed Extension Suite (CAPES), an upgrade destined for 350 USAF F-16Cs and F-16Ds modified under a $1.8 billion programme that included the APG-83 SABR.

When the USAF cancelled CAPES in March 2014 (except for the cockpit display element) due to sequestration (its funding was cut and priority given to production of the F-35A Lightning II), the Republic of Korea Air Force dropped its order in November. The US government also raised the price of the FMS sale by 45% to $760 million after the first two prototypes had been completed by BAE Systems at its facility in Fort Worth, Texas.

These two blows did not end Taiwan's requirement for an F-16 upgrade.

The $1.85 billion F-16 Viper upgrade programme was awarded to Lockheed Martin, as the prime contractor with the work carried out by AIDC in Taiwan in October 2012.

NORTHROP GRUMMAN APG-66 AND APG-68 RADARS

The first F-16A and F-16B models were equipped with the Westinghouse (now Northrop Grumman) APG-66 X-band radar. Using a slotted planar mechanically scanned array (MSA), it had four air-to-air and seven air-to-surface operating modes. The APG-66(V)2, fitted on Block 15 aircraft, introduced a more powerful signal processor, higher power output, improved reliability and increased range in cluttered or jamming conditions. The Mid-Life Update (MLU) programme introduced the upgraded APG-66(V)2A. Early versions remaining in service include the APG-66(V)3 on Block 20s.

F-16s are currently fitted with the Northrop Grumman APG-68(V) series (an evolution of the APG-66) with pulse Doppler range and angle track and a multimode MSA. Compared with the APG-66, the APG-68 has improved range, higher resolution and 25 operating modes. These include air-to-air modes for range-while-search, look-up search, velocity search with ranging, air combat, track-while-scan (up to ten targets), raid cluster resolution, single target track and pulse Doppler track to provide continuous-wave target illumination for Raytheon AIM-7 Sparrow missiles. Air-to-surface modes include ground-mapping, Doppler beam-sharpening, ground moving target, sea target, fixed-target track, target freeze after pop-up, beacon and air-to-ground ranging.

APG-68(V) was introduced on the Block 25 F-16C/F-16D in 1984, followed by the (V)4 version on Block 30s and the (V)6 during the production run of the Block 40. Initial Block 50 and Block 52 deliveries, starting in 1991, used the APG-68(V5) with an advanced VHSIC (very high-speed integrated circuit) programmable signal processor. International customers received the V(5), V(7) and V(8) versions.

The most advanced model of the APG-68 is the (V)9, which is installed on Block 50 and Block 52 aircraft. The V(9) provides 30% greater detection range, search volume,

"The most advanced model of the APG-68 is the (V)9, which provides 30% greater detection range, search volume, tracking accuracy, reliability and resolution, improved supportability and enhanced growth potential"

Test mechanics at Northrop Grumman with an F-16 nose radome for the company's CRJ flight testbed. Northrop Grumman

tracking accuracy, reliability and resolution, improved supportability and enhanced growth potential. Its advanced processing techniques provide enhanced electronic counter countermeasures (ECCM) capabilities and enable its synthetic aperture radar (SAR) mode to function correctly. The V(9) was upgraded after the Israeli Air Force reported problems with its performance.

The first production V(9) radars equipped the Hellenic Air Force Block 52+ aircraft delivered under the Peace Xenia IV programme.

NORTHROP GRUMMAN APG-83 RADAR

Northrop Grumman's APG-83 Scalable Agile Beam Radar (SABR) is defined as a multifunction, active electronically scanned array. It was developed as the replacement system for the legacy APG-68 type installed on countless USAF F-16s for the Radar Modernization Program (RMP).

According to the US government's Director of Operational Test and Evaluation (DOT&E), the APG-83 provides F-16 pilots with air-to-air and air-to-ground situational awareness, high-resolution synthetic aperture radar mapping, fire control and datalink support for air-to-air missiles. F-16 pilots use the APG-83 with onboard weapons, to accomplish the full kill chain against air, ground and surface targets from beyond visual range and in all weather conditions. Compared to the legacy APG-68 system, the APG-83 enables targeting and engagement from greater ranges with enhanced accuracy and combat identification.

According to Northrop Grumman, the APG-83 can operate in dense electronic environments and conduct simultaneous multi-mode operations. The radar unit is designed for installation as a form, fit and function modification that operates within the F-16's existing forward fuselage space with the original power and cooling capabilities without making any major modifications to the jet.

Northrop Grumman developed a liquid cooling system for the APG-83 which allowed Lockheed Martin to retain the same environmental cooling system used for the mechanically scanned radars fitted to earlier Block F-16 aircraft.

Implementation of the RMP sought to extend the operational viability and reliability of the F-16 and provides pilots with increased bandwidth that allows the aircraft to detect, track and identify greater numbers of targets faster and at greater distances, to counter and defeat increasingly sophisticated threats.

The APG-83 radar can be used for the suppression or destruction of enemy air defences, including targeting radars and surface-air-missiles.

DOT&E: AN OFFICIAL OVERVIEW

When the *DOT&E 2021 Annual Report* was published in January 2021, the US ANG (ANG) had already acquired and was fielding 72 APG-83 radars with an initial capability to meet a US Northern Command Joint Emergent Operational Need (JEON) for homeland defence. This initial JEON deployment was not under the oversight of the DOT&E, but included Phase 1 and Phase 2 developmental and operational testing of some APG-83 capabilities and reliability enhancements. The JEON programme was originally planned for completion in July 2021, but was delayed due to production issues.

Based on the JEON Phase 1 and Phase 2, the USAF approved the F-16 RMP to enter Phase 3 and Milestone C in March 2021. Milestone C is a review of a defence programme led by a Milestone Decision Authority (a team) at the end of the Engineering and Manufacturing Development phase of the defence acquisition process. Its purpose is to make a recommendation or seek approval to enter the programme into the production phase.

In Phase 1, the US ANG tested, fielded and acquired 24 radars to meet a US Northern Command Joint Emergent Operational Need Statement (JEONS) for homeland defence at the 113th FW, DC ANG. Phase 1 was completed in FY2020. In the follow-on Phase 2, the US ANG acquired 48 additional APG-83 radars. Phase 2 was completed in FY2022. Phase 3 developed the full APG-83 capability and the purchase of up to 450 radars for F-16 aircraft operated by the active-duty and the Air Force Reserve.

The RMP Program Office had directed a co-operative vulnerability investigation of the APG-83 radar installed in an F-16 aircraft assigned to the 40th Flight Test Squadron based at Eglin Air Force Base, Florida, in April 2022. Some parts of the required testing that could not be undertaken on an F-16 at Eglin were scheduled to be completed in laboratories by the 309th Software Engineering Group at Hill Air Force Base, Utah, in February 2023. An adversarial assessment was also planned to finish up the APG-83's IOT&E.

In January 2022, the DOT&E reported that operational testing of the APG-83 conducted by that date provided compelling evidence that it was a significant improvement over the legacy APG-68. That judgement was made despite the absence of some of the APG-83's required capabilities. At the time, the APG-83 was limited by the F-16's ageing mission computers, obsolete data system and insufficient network architecture. The upgrades of those sub-systems were either delayed or had failed to meet mission requirements. According to the DOT&E, the most significant upgrade was the transition from MIL-STD-1553 databuses to ethernet, part of the high-speed data network project.

In terms of suitability, the *DOT&E 2022 Annual Report* stated: "Early data suggests that the APG-83 will be suitable. Although

An airman secures a mid-body mounted wing to an AIM-120D AMRAAM missile. *USAF/CMSgt Glen Flanagan*

The array of a prototype APG-83 radar to be housed within an F-16 nose radome on Northrop Grumman's CRJ flight testbed. Northrop Grumman

the USAF has identified some maintenance challenges due to tight clearances between the radome and air data system, the radar has shown vast improvements in overall maintainability over the legacy APG-68. Pilots are generally satisfied with the human systems interface, although some limitations and trade-offs were required to integrate it with existing F-16 systems. The trade-offs result in increased pilot workload for some tasks, such as switching between different displays based on radar mode and function in use."

APG-83: THE STORY SO FAR

In a series of questions about the APG-83 radar submitted to Northrop Grumman, Mark Rossi, director of the SABR programme, said: "Northrop Grumman has been the sole radar provider for the F-16 for over four decades. The company has a history of keeping the F-16 relevant through technology upgrades of our mechanically scanned APG-66 and APG-68 radars. The APG-83 is a drop-in replacement of previous radars and moves this platform from the limitations of mechanically scanned radars to the simultaneous, multifunction capability of an AESA radar. The greater bandwidth, speed and agility of the APG-83 enables the F-16 to detect, track and identify a greater number of targets faster and at longer ranges, whether in the air or on the ground. The APG-83 AESA is a powerful upgrade to the previous M-scan, capable of operating in multiple modes including one for maritime search. It enables the F-16 to detect, track and identify a greater number of targets faster and at longer ranges than ever before."

In a USAF press release issued on July 2, 2020, following the first mission flown by four F-16Cs fitted with an APG-83 radar, Jack Harman, an F-16 test pilot assigned to the Eglin-based 40th Flight Test Squadron, said: "The APG-83's capability allows us to target the northwest corner of a small building or the cockpit of an aircraft from several miles away, beyond line-of-sight. The APG-83 improves our ability to identify a threat prior to us being targeted – we no longer must be inside a threat envelope to detect it."

By testing the four APG-83 radars at the same time, the Operational Flight Program Combined Test Force, comprising the 40th Flight Test Squadron and the 85th Test and Evaluation Squadron, was able to assess whether the aircraft experienced interference and could evaluate if the signal improved or degraded while operating together. The four-ship is the basic fighting formation of fighter aircraft, allowing the testers to see how the radar would respond in a combat scenario.

Detailing the APG-83's compatibility with the APG-81, Marc Rossi said: "The APG-83 system is over 90% compatible to Northrop Grumman's APG-81 AESA radar, which equips F-35 Lightning II stealth fighters and uses the electronic protection capabilities of the APG-81."

As an insight into the functionality of the APG-83 radar, it's worth taking a quick look at the APG-81. In terms of type, the APG-81 is a pulse Doppler radar system that runs multiple waveforms for air-to-air and air-to-ground. The front end of the radar comprises the array, the T/R modules and the radiating element. It is bolted directly to the integrated forebody and positioned up front in the radome.

The APG-81 has an electronically steered array controlled by a computer with no mechanical motion. Designed as a multi-mode system, it has 32 modes of operation: 12 air-to-air, 12 air-to-ground (including two maritime modes: ship target track and sea search), four electronic warfare (electronic attack and electronic protection), two navigation and two weather modes. Some of the modes are high resolution and are supported by the sophisticated signal processing.

TESTING THE APG-83

Northrop Grumman flew an APG-83 radar installed on an F-16 for the first time in 2009. Explaining the consecutive test phases of

Load crew transport an AIM-9X Sidewinder suspended on an MJ-1 lift truck. US ANG/Captain Rebecca Roodhouse

the APG-83, Marc Rossi said: "There was a series of testing procedures for the APG-83 that varied depending on the development stage of the radar. When first developed, the APG-83 went through a series of development lab testing from integration to quality. As the APG-83 evolved, the radar system went through extensive flight testing on the company's CRJ aircraft. By using the CRJ, Northrop Grumman was able to replicate the installation conditions of the F-16 for the purposes of testing. The CRJ's standard nose was removed, the APG-83 radar was configured onto the front of the aircraft and then a replica of an F-16 nose was installed on the CRJ. This allowed us to test and collect data from the radar that should mimic what an F-16 pilot will see. Each radar system was also tested for operational functionality and then flight tested each time there was a software update. The APG-83 is software defined and hardware enabled, which speeds up development time and eliminates reconfiguring hardware for every upgrade. Customer changes and upgrades can be completed through software integration only."

Describing the integration effort for the APG-83 on an F-16, Rossi described the APG-83 as a drop-in replacement radar for Northrop Grumman's mechanically scanned radar: "We were able to use our flight proven knowledge and understanding of the F-16 to create the APG-83. Installation was simple as the radar was intended to fit perfectly with the F-16's current design in terms of both electronic and physical connections. For example, the APG-83 has its own liquid cooling system that is completely self-contained to the radar – think of it as a

"The JEON programme was originally planned for completion in July 2021, but was delayed due to production issues"

Weapon loaders assigned to the 35th Maintenance Group attach an AGM-88 HARM missile onto an F-16 at Misawa Air Base, Japan. USAF/Airman 1st Class Leon Redfern

more advanced version of a car radiator. The coolant is chilled by an existing system on the aircraft, so no additional modifications were needed."

Because of the company's prior knowledge of the aircraft, Northrop Grumman can retrofit the APG-83 in less than a week. The new F-16 radar is being installed at military bases throughout the USs and around the world. Many are installed in country by local representatives and contractors to meet the specific needs of that customer.

The USAF made a full-rate production decision for the APG-83 RADAR in September 2024.

AAQ-13 AND AAQ-14 LANTIRN PODS

The Lockheed Martin (originally Martin Marietta) Low-Altitude Navigation and Targeting Infrared for Night (LANTIRN) system was originally developed in the 1980s. It was the first and most widely produced targeting and navigation pod used by the F-16 and 1,400 are in service with ten countries.

LANTIRN provides an all-weather capability for weapons delivery. It is a unique system that provides terrain-following capability for high-speed, low-altitude all-weather operations. It's a twin-pod system, combining the AAQ-13 navigation pod and AAQ-14 targeting pod. It was introduced into USAF service in 1987 and equipped some USAF F-16s during Operation Desert Storm in 1991, its first major combat use. Since then, it has been widely used and integrated with multiple aircraft types.

The AAQ-13 navigation pod provides high-speed, low-altitude precision attack capability with a wide field-of-view forward-looking infrared (FLIR) sensor and Raytheon's Ku-band terrain-following radar (TFR). The two sensors provide a picture displayed on the pilot's head-up display (HUD) and adequate night vision for safe low-level flying. The AAQ-13 is linked to the aircraft's control system in terrain-following mode to

ensure it stays at a pre-set altitude above the ground. The TFR capability is not available in some export versions, designated the AAQ-20 Pathfinder.

The AAQ-14 targeting pod contains a stabilised wide and narrow field-of-view FLIR sensor for day/night target acquisition and targeting of precision-guided weapons with a laser designator and rangefinder. The pod is designed with a maximum operating altitude of 25,000ft. The pilot uses the AAQ-14 to detect a target with the FLIR's wide field-of-view function cued by the radar or an off-board sensor to point it in the right direction. Once the target is acquired, the pilot switches to the narrow field-of-view mode to identify and engage. The AAQ-14's capability was further improved with the M6.5 Operational Flight Program (OFP) software installed on F-16 Mid-Life Update (MLU) aircraft starting in 2014.

The AAQ-19 Pathfinder version has been exported without the capability to designate AGM-65 Maverick air-to-surface missiles and lacks some air-to-air operating modes.

AAQ-28 LITENING TARGETING POD

The original Litening pod, designed by Israel's Rafael in the early 1990s, is the most widely used precision, day/night navigation and targeting pod. It won the US Precision Attack Targeting System competition in 1998 and 168 pods were ordered for ANG and Air Force Reserve Command F-16s. The system was fielded in 1999 as the AAQ-28(V)1, the first in a series adopted by the US military. Northrop Grumman, the licence holder for US production, upgraded the system to (V)2 standard by incorporating an improved FLIR, laser target marker and updated software.

The AAQ-28(V)3 Litening Extended Range (ER) version, fielded in 2001, included a FLIR with increased range and greater resolution. The AAQ-28(V)6 Litening Advanced Technology (AT) version, fielded in 2003, provided even greater range, accurate target co-ordinate generation and multi-target cueing.

The Litening Generation Four (G4) was first delivered to the USAF in 2008. It features an improved mid-wave FLIR, a new laser illuminator, two CCD TV sensors (one with wide and one with narrow field-of-view), a laser spot tracker and an infrared laser marker. It has improved target recognition capabilities resulting from the incorporation of the laser target-imaging programme, including short-wave infrared laser-augmented imaging. This enhances the ability to capture images in conditions where the medium-wave infrared FLIR and CCD are less effective. The first international deliveries were to Denmark.

The AAQ-28(V)7 and (V)9 Litening Sensor Enhancement (SE) versions, featuring a

The AGM-88 HARM missile designed to seek and destroy enemy radar-equipped air defence systems. USAF

> **"LANTIRN was the first and most widely produced targeting and navigation pod used by the F-16 and 1,400 are in service with ten countries"**

two-way digital datalink, were ordered by the USAF as one of the two winning designs in a 2010 competition. In 2014, the air force started to upgrade its (V)1 and (V)2 versions to (V)7 standard.

The Rafael-produced Litening G4 Advanced with an air-to-air capability features 1K x 1K FLIR and CCD sensors for superior high-definition imagery. The G4 enables precise long-range target detection, identification and tracking for combat aircraft, featuring advanced laser colour imaging, and datalink capabilities. The G4 pod incorporates a short-wave infrared (SWIR) laser imaging sensor, laser spot tracker and laser marker/designator for precision-guided weapon delivery. The first G4 pods entered service with the USAF in 2008.

AAQ-33 SNIPER TARGETING POD

The Lockheed Martin Sniper advanced targeting pod was first ordered by the USAF in 2001. The single-pod system was integrated on the F-16 with the M4 OFP software installed between 2005 (the year Sniper entered operational service) and 2007. The pod features a third-generation, mid-wavelength FLIR, a high-definition dual field-of-view CCD TV and a laser target designator, spot tracker, rangefinder, auto-tracking of moving targets and, perhaps most significantly, a two-way Link 16-compatible datalink that feeds imagery and streaming video to other aircraft or ground units. This datalink capability entered USAF service with the M4.2 OFP in 2007.

AIM-9X SIDEWINDER

The AIM-9X Sidewinder is a supersonic air-to-air guided missile with full day/night capability, missile body, a passive infrared (IR) target acquisition system, proportional navigational guidance, a closed-loop position fin actuator unit (FAU) and a target detector, warhead and rocket motor. It's powered by a solid propellant rocket motor that incorporates a manual safe-arm selector assembly. The missile is configured with an annular blast fragmentation warhead controlled by an electronic safe-arm device.

Aerodynamic lift and stability are provided by four forward-mounted fixed wings. Four fins, mounted in line with the fixed wings and activated by the FAU, control the missile in flight. Manoeuvrability is enhanced by a jet vane control (JVC) that deflects the rocket motor thrust to aid turning, which is controlled by a tail actuation section for extreme agility in close-range, high-G combat.

A key benefit of the AIM-9X is its imaging focal plane array infrared sensor, which has IR-counter countermeasures and has demonstrated highly effective detection and tracking performance within visual and BVR engagement. It also incorporates improvements integrated as part its spiral development. The Block II version includes improved fuse and updated electronics – which enable lock-on after launch capability

The pilot of an F-16C releases an AGM-154 JSOW air-to-ground guided weapon over the Utah Test and Training Range during a Combat Hammer Weapons System Evaluation Program mission. USAF/MSgt Michael Ammons

and BVR engagements – including the use of a datalink. This capability means the pilot can take full advantage of the aerodynamic performance of the AIM-9X. The ongoing test programme, which was nearing completion at the end of 2013, demonstrated excellent results of 17 kills for 21 test shots.

In late 2012, Raytheon was awarded a development contract for the Block III – the next evolution of the Sidewinder – which mated the Block II seeker and datalink advances with an improved rocket motor, new internal systems and warhead. The Block II offers up to 60% more range and greater capability, giving the F-16 a potent air-to-air missile. Later Block AIM-9Xs incorporate a reprogrammable computer to adjust for new IR countermeasure challenges. The AIM-9X entered service in November 2003 with the USAF, where the lead platform was the F-15C, and the US Navy, where the lead platform was the F/A-18C Hornet.

More than 21,800 AIM-9X missiles have been produced or planned across all variants, with production accelerating to 2,500 units annually as of June 2025. This includes 1,289 Block I missiles and over 11,635 Block II/II+ missiles delivered to the US and allied nations.

The AIM-9X missile measures 119in long, weighs 188lb, has a 5in diameter and wings and fi ns with spans of 13.9in and 17.5in, respectively.

AIM-120 AMRAAM MISSILE

The F-16's primary air-to-air weapon is the Raytheon AIM-120 AMRAAM beyond visual range (BVR) radar-guided missile. The AIM-120 has four fixed mid-body mounted wings, four electric motor-driven movable tailfins and an umbilical connection enabling communication with the aircraft for targeting and initialisation. The missile consists of four sections: guidance, armament, propulsion and control. The hardware and software necessary for target acquisition and tracking, navigation, datalink processing and electrical power distribution is fitted in the guidance section. Seeker/servo electronics, a transmitter/electrical conversion unit (ECU), an electronics unit, an inertial reference unit (IRU) and a quad/target detection device (QTDD) are also housed in the guidance section, with antennas for the QTDD mounted in the aft portion.

AMRAAM uses a radar proximity fuse which activates the high-explosive fragmentation warhead at a pre-set distance from the target. The missile is configured with a single boost-sustain, reduced-smoke hydroxyl terminated polybutadiene solid propellant encased in an insulated steel case, which is an integral part of the airframe. Control electronics, actuator batteries and four independently controlled servo actuators are the main components of the control section.

The latest version of the AMRAAM, the AIM-120D, was developed to add new capabilities to the AIM-120C7. A two-way

A munitions troop tightens a screw on a GBU-12 Paveway II fitted with a standard nose-mounted laser seeker. USAF/Senior Airman Joao Marcus Costa

datalink, GPS navigation, increased electronic protection and improved range make it the most advanced air-to-air weapon in service today. It has improved kinematics due to a longer battery life and so runs for longer, high off-boresight capability because of improved algorithms that control the flight trajectory more accurately as it homes in on the target, with GPS for better accuracy as it gets further along its trajectory.

The initial operational test (OT) of the AIM-120D finished in 2014. The missile was subsequently declared combat-ready by the US Navy in January 2015 and the USAF in July 2015. Performance results from the OT remain classified but those deemed the most impressive are believed to include the improved trajectory during the missile's terminal stage when approaching its target and a greater range to target gained from the extended battery life.

Over 14,000 AMRAAMs of all types have been manufactured. The latest AIM-120D-3 version is in active production with contracts for Lots 39 and 40 awarded in August 2025. Raytheon currently manufactures 1,400 AIM-120 missiles per year. According to a Raytheon spokesperson, the company has established an AMRAAM road map with the USAF comprising regular software improvements designed to counter future air-to-air threats. The AIM-120C missile is 144in long, weighs 356lb, has a 7in diameter, wings and fins with spans of 17.5in and a blast-fragmentation warhead of 45lb.

AGM-65 MAVERICK

The AGM-65 Maverick is an air-to-ground missile designed for close air support, air interdiction and suppression of enemy air defences with a lock-on before launch day/night capability. It consists of three sections: a guidance package, a warhead and a rocket motor in a cylindrical body with long-chord delta wings and tail control surfaces. The Maverick can be fitted with three different seekers: electro-optical (AGM-65B), imaging infrared (AGM-65D) and laser (AGM-65E) and it can be armed with either a 125lb shape-charged warhead with a contact fuse or a 300lb penetrator with a delayed-fuse. The solid-rocket motor is common to all variants. It measures 97.7in long and has a fuselage diameter of 12in. The AGM-65B weighs 462lb, the AGM-65D is 485lb – both weights include the 125lb shaped-charge warhead – while the AGM-65E weighs 628lb including a 300lb penetrator warhead.

AGM-88 HIGH-SPEED ANTI-RADIATION MISSILE (HARM)

The AGM-88 HARM is a supersonic air-to-ground missile designed to seek and destroy enemy radar-equipped air defence systems. This includes emissions from surface-to-air missiles, radar gathered anti-aircraft artillery and any type of radar or electronic waveform. It is equipped with an inertial and GPS guidance system that homes in on radar emissions through a fixed antenna

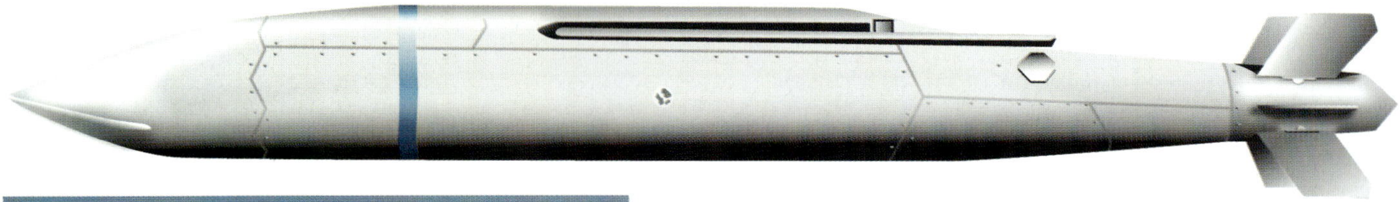

The AGM-154 JSOW GPS/INS-guided air-to-surface glide weapon. USAF

An F-16D drops a GBU-24 Paveway II over the Utah Test and Training Range during a Combat Hammer Weapons System Evaluation Program mission from Hill Air Force Base, Utah. USAF/86th Fighter Weapons Squadron

and seeker head in the missile nose. Each consists of four sections: a passive broadband radio frequency guidance section, a direct fragmentation, variable charge-to-metal warhead, an electro-mechanical wing control section and a smokeless, solid-propellant, dual-thrust rocket motor.

The USAF primarily uses the AGM-88C, but Raytheon is currently producing the HARM Control Section Modification (HCSM) which incorporates a GPS/INS digital flight computer for precision targeting. This means if an emitter shuts down, the missile can continue to the target using the GPS co-ordinates, overcoming a targeting issue faced by legacy missiles that only guide on emissions from the target threat.

The HCSM is retrofitted to existing AGM-88C missiles by Raytheon. The modification involves removal of the original control section and installation of a GPS/INS digital flight computer with new software to transform the old missile into a precision-guided AGM-88F. The original seeker, guidance section (located in the front of the missile) and solid-propellant, dual-thrust rocket motor remain unchanged.

The modified HARM also allows the pilot to designate a missile impact zone, zones of exclusion and areas in which the missile must not fly. Bill Reaves, senior manager for business development SEAD/DEAD, said: "In a nutshell, it allows the pilot more control of the missile impact point – where it can hit and where it can't – which reduces the likelihood of collateral damage and provides the ability to counter target shutdown."

The AGM-88 is 164in long, has a fuselage diameter of 10in and weighs 780-810lb, including a 143.5lb warhead.

KEY AGM-88 VARIANTS

AGM-88C The primary current production variant, featuring an upgraded blast-fragmentation warhead and improved guidance

AGM-88D and AGM-88E advanced anti-radiation guided missile(AARGM) Incorporates GPS/INS and a millimetre-wave active radar seeker for terminal guidance, which enables engagement even if the target radar is turned off

AGM-88F HARM control section modification (HCSM) Adds GPS/INS capability to older AGM-88B or AGM-88C models for increased precision

AGM-88G AARGM extended range (ER) A significantly upgraded version with a new rocket motor with double the range, designed for internal carriage on F-35 Lightning IIs

AGM-154 JOINT STAND-OFF WEAPON (JSOW)

The AGM-154 JSOW is a 1,000lb-class, low-observable, INS/GPS-guided family of air-to-surface glide weapons with all-weather, day/night capability. It consists of a common airframe and avionics providing for a modular payload assembly to attack stationary or moving targets.

Once released, the JSOW is an unpowered glide bomb with a range from 15-60+ miles, which enables the attacking aircraft to remain outside the range of point and short-range air defence systems. After launch, folding wings extend and the weapon flies a pre-programmed flight path before dispensing its payload over the intended target. The AGM-154C version features an infrared terminal seeker and carries a 500lb two-stage Broach penetrator warhead to attack hardened targets.

The AGM-154 is 160in long, has a fuselage diameter of 13in and a wingspan of 106in.

KEY AGM-154 JSOW VARIANTS

AGM-154A Carries 145 BLU-97/B combined effects munitions for deployment against area targets such as troops, vehicles and SAM sites using GPS-aided inertial guidance

AGM-154A-1 An export/modified version replacing the submunitions with a 500lb BLU-111 warhead for reduced collateral damage

AGM-154B Carries six BLU-108/B canisters designed to each release four anti-armour submunitions for moving targets

AGM-154C-1 JSOW Block III A modified, network-enabled version of the C variant, with an autonomous target acquisition (ATA) capability, featuring a Link-16 weapon datalink for targeting moving maritime or land targets

GBU-12 PAVEWAY II

The GBU-12 Paveway II is a 500lb laser-guided bomb that uses the Mk82/BLU-111 blast fragmentation warhead. It has large guidance fins attached to the front of the high-explosive bomb body and folding wings (the air foil group) which open on release for stability and increased manoeuvrability.

When dropped, the GBU-12's nose-mounted semi-active laser seeker tracks the laser spot on the target provided by the F-16's targeting pod, a forward air controller or an unmanned air vehicle. During flight, bomb fins move to ensure accurate impact on the target. The Paveway II has 'bang-bang mode guidance'.

The GBU-12 is 131in long, weighs 606lb, has a warhead diameter of 10.75in and an airfoil diameter of 18in.

GBU-10 PAVEWAY II

The GBU-10 Paveway II is a 2,000lb laser-guided bomb that uses the Mk84/BLU-117 blast fragmentation warhead.

It measures 169.9in long, weighs 2,110lb, has a warhead diameter of 10.75in and a diameter of 18in.

GBU-24 PAVEWAY II

The GBU-24 Paveway II is a 2,000lb laser-guided penetration bomb comprising five major sections: a nose-mounted laser

A weapons team building a GBU-31 JDAM training munition at Eglin Air Force Base, Florida. USAF/Samuel King Jr

A weapon loads team moves an AGM-154 JSOW into place under the wing of an F-16C at Eglin Air Force Base, Florida. USAF/Samuel King Jr

guidance and control unit and tail assembly, an airfoil group, an adapter group, a bomb fuse and a warhead. Target designation uses a pulse-coding system that feeds the same data to the seeker and the designator, a function designed to only kill the intended target. GBU-24-series munitions carry hard target penetrator warheads: a GBU-24B/B has a BLU-109A/B, while a GBU-24E/B carries a BLU-109A/B or a BLU-116A/B.

The GBU-24/B is 172.7in long, weighs 2,256lb and has a diameter of 18in. Another version, the GBU-24A/B, uses the BLU-109 hard target penetrator warhead, is 169.6in long, weighs 2,372lb, has a diameter of 14.5in and a fin span of 81.6in when deployed.

A BRU-61/A carriage system loaded with 250lb-class GBU-39/B precision glide weapons. USAF

GBU-31 JOINT DIRECT ATTACK MUNITION (JDAM)

The JDAM is a guidance set of which there is a series – designated KMU-556, KMU-557 and KMU-558 – that converts existing unguided free-fall 2,000lb-class warheads into accurate all-weather munitions. Each different guidance set consists of a tail kit fitted with an INS/GPS receiver, a battery, a set of aerosurfaces (moving fins) to provide lift and an umbilical cover. The tail kit, which also houses selective availability anti-spoofing modules, is bolted to one of four different types of 2,000lb-class warhead, the Mk84, the BLU-109 hard target-penetrator or the BLU-117 and BLU-119 blast fragmentation versions.

"The modified HARM allows the pilot to designate a missile impact zone, zones of exclusion and areas in which the missile must not fly"

A GBU-31 JDAM can be launched from different altitudes from very low to very high and from different delivery profiles: a dive, toss-and-loft or in straight-and-level flight. Depending on the aircraft launch speed and altitude, the GBU-31 has a range of up to 15 miles.

The GBU-31's specifications depend on the warhead. The Mk84 GBU-31(V)1 is 152.7in long, weighs 2,039lb and has a warhead diameter of 25in. A BLU-109 GBU-31(V)3 is 148.6in long, weighs 2,118lb and has a warhead diameter of 25in.

A BLU-119 GBU-31(V)5 measures 152.7in long, weighs 2,059lb and has a warhead diameter of 25in.

GBU-39/B SMALL DIAMETER BOMB (SDB)

The GBU-39/B is a 250lb-class autonomous conventional air-to-ground precision glide weapon designed for striking fixed and stationary re-locatable targets from stand-off range. It consists of the weapon and the BRU-61/A four-place miniature munition pneumatic carriage system. An advanced anti-jam GPS-aided INS provides guidance to the co-ordinates of a stationary target. It has a multi-purpose penetrating/blast fragmentation warhead coupled with a cockpit-selectable electronic fuse. A proximity sensor provides a height of burst capability. After launch, the wings deploy and it glides to the target using GPS guidance up to a range of more than 60 miles.

The GBU-39 measures 70.8in long and 7.5in wide, has a wingspan of 152.4in and weighs 285lb.

ADM-160C MINIATURE AIR-LAUNCHED DECOY JAMMER (MALD-J)

The MALD-J is an air-launched, expendable decoy/jammer designed to deceive, saturate and obstruct an enemy integrated air defence system, but is technically a missile. It is classed as a stand-in jammer and requires much less power than the stand-off systems integrated on the EA-18G Growler. Its low power requirement is sufficient for the jamming role because the missile can operate much closer to a target.

The ADM-160C comprises a forward payload section housing the electronic warfare elements and a larger aft section, aft-mounted actuator control fins and a variable sweep wing assembly. The decoy's intent is to deceive the adversary into concentrating its assets into a pointless engagement. MALD-J achieves this thanks to the signature augmentation system (SAS), which uses active radar enhancers operating across a broad range of frequencies to mimic the radar signature of various combat aircraft.

The ADM-160C MALD-J passed operational tests on the B-52H and F-16 in April 2014, then moved from low-rate initial production to full-rate production. Raytheon delivered the 1,000th MALD in May 2014 and signed a contract in March 2015 for production Lot 8, which was part of a two-year agreement, followed by a contract option for Lot 10 in 2016 and a follow-on Lot 11 contract for 250 weapons in 2018.

The USAF demonstrated in-flight retargeting capabilities and integrated a GPS-aided inertial navigation system (GAINS II) to improve the MALD-J's navigational accuracy in GPS-denied environments. In 2018, a subsequent version dubbed MALD-X successfully demonstrated low-level flight capabilities, improved EW payload and enhanced datalinks.

The ADM-160C measures 113in long, has an 11in wide fuselage, a wingspan of 67in and weighs 282lb.

Fifty Years and

Insight into Pratt & Whitney's F100 family of turbofan engines, the power behind the F-16.

When the Pratt & Whitney F100 first entered service on the McDonnell Douglas F-15A Eagle in 1972, one would have been bold to forecast that it would become the west's most successful and safest fourth-generation turbofan fighter engine.

Developed in the late 1960s to compete for the joint USAF-US Navy advanced turbine gas generator fighter engine requirement for the new F-15 and F-14 Tomcat air-superiority fighters, the Pratt & Whitney F100-PW-100 was first selected for the twin-engine F-15.

It powered the first flight of the F-15 in July 1972 and production F-15A Eagles when they began entering service with the USAF in February 1974. The US Navy initially chose to engine its F-14s with a version of the P&W TF30 that powered USAF and Royal Australian Air Force F-111 strike aircraft. However, after more than a decade of Tomcat service with TF30 engines, the navy decided to replace the TF30s with more powerful GE Aviation F110-400s.

In terms of reliability, the USAF's early experience with the F100-100 was not encouraging. In operational service, the engine demonstrated high levels of wear and has a tendency to stall, while afterburners often failed to start or extinguished too soon. These afterburner flame-outs produced sizeable jets of fuel in the engines' exhaust nozzles and the jets were ignited by hot exhaust gases, creating waves of high gas pressure. The waves backed up into the engines, causing them to stall.

Also underwhelming was the USAF's P&W F100-200 engine selected to power the F-16 Fighting Falcon for its first flight in January 1974 and its entry into service in January 1979.

When both F100 versions entered service – each offered a little less than 24,000lb of maximum thrust with reheat – they were only good for about 900 total accumulated cycles (TACs) of operation between major overhauls.

MORE MODULAR

Nevertheless, the F100-100 and F100-200 revolutionised fighter-engine design in terms of engine modularity and relative ease of maintenance, according to Jeff Zotti, director of Pratt & Whitney's F100, J52 and TF33 programmes. While displaying conventional engine architecture – the F100 has three fan stages, ten compressor stages, an annular combustor, two high-pressure turbine [HPT] stages, two low-pressure turbine stages and an exhaust nozzle) – the F100 was designed so that any one of its major modules was removable and replaceable on an operational air base rather than at the maintenance depot.

Zotti explained: "You do have to remove the engine from the aircraft before any individual module can be removed." But the F100's fan, core, low-pressure turbine, exhaust nozzle and gearbox could all be removed and replaced separately without having to disassemble the rest of the engine – "a unique characteristic" according to Zotti.

The USAF found the F100's reliability and durability poor for nearly a decade, giving P&W a major challenge. However, when the air force introduced its Alternative Fighter Engine programme in 1983 – which spurred development of the GE Aviation F110 as an alternative engine for the F-15 and F-16 – P&W responded well by developing the F100-220.

F100-PW-220 AND F100-PW-229

This upgraded engine offered substantially increased reliability, durability and stability by introducing improved compressor aerodynamics and cooling efficiency, along with more effective delivery of compressor bleed cooling air to the engine's hot section. These improvements gave the F100-220 a service life of 4,300 TACs between overhauls, equivalent to roughly seven years of on-wing time. Its maximum dry thrust remained at 14,590lb and its maximum wet thrust with afterburner at 23,770lb.

A cutaway of a Pratt & Whitney F100-PW-229 engine. Pratt & Whitney

30 Million Hours

The Pratt & Whitney F100-PW-229 engine is rated at 29,160lb of thrust. Pratt & Whitney

The F100-220 also introduced another major upgrade, aimed at enhancing engine safety and reliability. Although the F100-200 retained the F100's traditional hydromechanical control system as a back-up, P&W gave the F100-220 a digital electronic engine control, along with an engine diagnostic unit to record in-flight engine performance data for maintenance and troubleshooting faults. This big step in innovation allowed pilots of F100-powered aircraft to command unrestricted throttle movement and reduced their workload. When introducing the upgrades into new F100-220 engines, P&W also began producing F100-220E conversion kits so any previously built F100-100 and F100-200 could be converted to F100-220 standard.

P&W's next step in developing the F100 was to introduce the F100-229 in 1989.

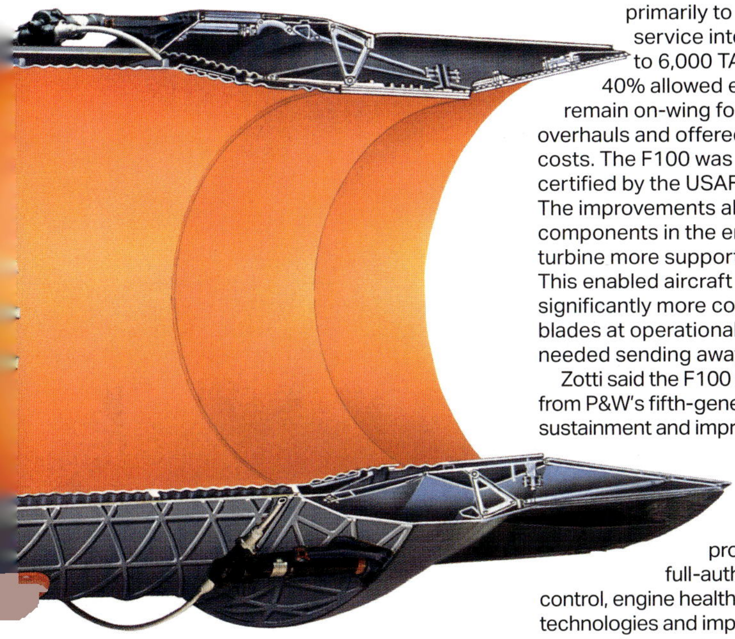

This engine, incorporated a new suite of durability advancements, among them new coatings for its HPT stages, and offered a dry thrust increase to 17,800lb and maximum thrust with reheat of 29,160lb.

The F100-229, comparable in thrust to GE's F110-129 models, remains the standard F100 model offered for the F-16C, F-16D and F-15E Strike Eagle. However, in 2009, P&W began offering an F100-229 engine enhancement package (EEP), which parlayed technological advances developed for P&W's fifth-generation F119 and F135 fighter engines into a new suite of improvements for the F100.

F100-PW-229EEP

These improvements, which included thermal barrier coatings and advanced materials in the F110-229EEP's combustor and HPT, were primarily to increase the engine's service interval between overhauls to 6,000 TACS. This increase of 40% allowed each F100-229EEP to remain on-wing for up to ten years between overhauls and offered 30% lower life-cycle costs. The F100 was the first fighter engine certified by the USAF for a 6,000-TAC interval. The improvements also aimed to make "the components in the engine's compressor and turbine more supportable," according to Zotti. This enabled aircraft mechanics to replace significantly more compressor and turbine blades at operational bases, so fewer engines needed sending away for depot maintenance.

Zotti said the F100 continues to benefit from P&W's fifth-generation F119 and F135 sustainment and improvement programmes: "It's the only fourth-generation engine that can learn from two operational fifth generation products." In addition to full-authority digital engine control, engine health monitoring and sensor technologies and improved turbine coatings, the F100 programme also work on more damage-tolerant materials and advanced cooling schemes.

However, P&W's fifth-generation engines have also benefitted from the F100 programme and continue to do so. These benefits are not necessarily from new technologies, said Zotti: "From early on, we learned what worked and what didn't work [in providing customer technical and logistical support]"and how to support a mixed-model family, in a variety of configurations, and a large customer base."

P&W's support for the F100 includes a continuous component improvement programme, which is funded by the engine family's many customers. "[On their behalf] we look at reliability and maintainability drivers and Pratt & Whitney looks at ways of improving the design," said Zotti.

Over time, P&W's improvements have made the F100 a major sales success. The company has now made more than 7,300 F100s, of which more than 3,900 remain in service. Zotti said P&W "supports the air forces of 23 countries" in operating F100 engines. Its latest customer is Romania, which purchased a batch of F-16s secondhand from Portugal. Another new customer is the Iraqi Air Force, which bought 36 Block 52 F-16IQs.

Interest in the F100 is "from new customers, as well as existing customers who want to expand their fleets," said Zotti, who thinks "there will be F100s in service for at least another 20 years." Not only is this because

> **"The USAF found the F100's reliability and durability poor for nearly a decade, giving P&W a major challenge."**

A Pratt & Whitney F100-PW-229 engine undergoing pre-delivery inspection. Pratt & Whitney

A Pratt & Whitney F100-PW-229 engine in afterburner during a ground test. Pratt & Whitney

some customers plan to operate their F-16s for at least the next 20-25 years, but also because P&W doesn't see the F-15 being replaced any time soon.

A PLACE IN HISTORY

According to USAF statistics, the F100 is the safest US single fighter engine ever made. It has also made history many times. On July 10, 2013, the first arrested landing on an aircraft carrier by an unmanned aircraft was accomplished by an F100-powered Northrop Grumman X-47B, which landed on the deck of the USS *George HW Bush* (CVN 77). For this achievement Northrop Grumman, the US Navy and the X-47B development team won the National Aeronautic Association's 2013 Robert J Collier Trophy, US aviation's most prestigious award. On April 22, 2015, off the coast of Maryland, the same aircraft-engine combination successfully conducted the world's first fully autonomous aerial refuelling.

F100 CONTRACTS

On July 16, 2018, Pratt & Whitney announced that its F100 engine had reached 28 million engine flight hours – a major milestone for an engine that powers more than 2,000 aircraft around the world.

Since its entry into military service in 1972, the F100 has an unmatched record of safety with the lowest non-recoverable in-flight shutdowns in its class. The latest configuration F100-PW-229 engine, in service for more than 30 years, has zero Class A mishaps since initial operation.

On July 27, 2022, Pratt & Whitney commemorated 50 years of trusted and reliable service for the F100 engine, which at that point had accumulated more than 30 million engine flight hours, one of several significant milestones:

1972 The Pratt & Whitney F100-PW-100 powersd the F-15 Eagle's first flight on July 27

1983 The USAF Thunderbirds demonstration team transitions to F100-PW-200-powered F-16 aircraft. The engine remains the exclusive

An aerospace propulsion technician inspects an F100 turbofan engine at Holloman Air Force Base, New Mexico USAF/Airman 1st Class Isaiah Pedrazzini

Airmen assigned to the 49th Component Maintenance Squadron conduct a test run on an F100 engine USAF/Airman 1st Class Isaiah Pedrazzini

The 49th Component Maintenance Squadron inspects the oil on a F100 USAF/Airman 1st Class Isaiah Pedrazzini

On February 13, 2024, Pratt & Whitney announced it had won an F100 engine performance-based logistics (PBL) sustainment contract from the Republic of Korea's Defense Acquisition Program Administration (DAPA). Valued at $355 million, the contract was the third consecutive PBL contract that Pratt & Whitney and DAPA had signed since 2012, offering ongoing maintenance support for Korea's F-15s and F-16s. The contract is supporting more efficient depot planning and is improving overall fleet readiness through long-term material forecasting.

On July 23, 2024, Pratt & Whitney announced the delivery of the first of several F100 engines to Poland in support of ongoing efforts to strengthen the readiness of its F-16 fleet. The F100 engines powering the Polish F-16 fleet were manufactured at Pratt & Whitney's Rzeszów facility. Today, nearly 20 years later, the Rzeszów facility produces static structures and critical rotating parts for the unit.

On October 1, 2024, Pratt & Whitney celebrated the opening of its new $255 million, 845,000ft^2 facility in Oklahoma City, the company's largest military engines field location. It enables Pratt & Whitney to meet the growing demands for US and foreign operators of the F135, F117, TF33, F100 and F119 engines.Discussing the opening, VP Greg Treacy said: "This expansion more than doubles our footprint in Oklahoma City, ensuring we have the capacity and agility to support increased workloads as military programmes ramp up and new ones come online."

The site features automation and advanced technologies that will streamline processes, improving accuracy, speed and cost-effectiveness, supporting engines for the B-52, C-17, E-3, F-15, F-16, F-22 and F-35.

On November 14, 2025, Pratt & Whitney announced it has received a $1.09 billion contract from the Defense Logistics Agency (Aviation) to provide consumable and depot-level repairable parts for the F100 afterburning turbofan engine. The contract includes a five-year base period and an option for an additional five years, allowing work to continue through 2035 if all options are exercised.

propulsion provider for the team, with the F100-PW-229 powering the current aircraft

1985 The F100-PW-220 fields the first digital electronic control in 1985, which delivers extremely smooth control scheduling to provide pilots the exact power settings they need to optimise performance.

1989 The upgraded F100-PW-229 variant, featuring advanced avionics and increased thrust, conducted its first flight and remains in production today

2006 The F100-PW-229 is the first fighter engine to increase engine depot maintenance interval to 6,000 TACs, effectively extending the typical depot interval from 7-10 years, while providing a 30% life-cycle cost reduction over the life of the engine.

2022 The latest F100 variants incorporate fifth-generation technologies such as advanced thermal coatings, improved turbine cooling capabilities, prognostics and engine health monitoring features.

An F100 is inspected at Nellis Air Force Base, Nevada USAF/Airman 1st Class Heather Amador Paulino

Constant Improvement

Insight to GE Aviation's F110 family of turbofan engines.

Originally developed in the early 1980s for the US Navy to offer a much higher-thrust alternative for the insufficiently powerful Pratt & Whitney TF30-P-414As powering the navy's F-14A Tomcats, GE Aviation's F110 engine began life as the F101X, a derivative of the F101-102 turbofan developed for the Rockwell B-1B bomber. Renamed the F110, its core is virtually identical to the B-1B's F101-102, the KC-135's CFM56-2 and the B-2's F118-101. Its developmental maturity and thrust capability to break the monopoly on US fighter aircraft that Pratt & Whitney had secured in the 1970s.

The USAF had launched its Alternative Fighter Engine programme (known in US military circles as 'The Great Engine War') in 1984. The aim was to find an engine that not only could reduce maintenance costs compared with the P&W F100-100 and F100-200 engines powering the USAF's F-15s and F-16s, but also provide more thrust.

The GE Aviation F110-GE-129 turbofan engine rated at 29,000lb of thrust is subject to a Component Improvement Programme. GE Aviation

P&W's early F100-100 engines offered only 900 total accumulated cycles (TACs) between overhauls and the USAF also regarded the F100-200 as being insufficiently reliable. While P&W later fixed these problems with the F100-220, it did so in the knowledge that the GE F110 was winning volume orders on the F-16 and F-15E Strike Eagle and offered 3,000 TACs on-wing before overhaul.

GE made the F110 available initially to the USAF as the F110-100, which provided 28,000lb of thrust with reheat for Block 30 and Block 40 F-16s, and as the F110-400 for the US Navy, which offered a similar thrust level for the F-14B and F-14D.

The F110 had three fan stages, nine high-pressure compressor stages, an annular combustor, a single high-pressure turbine stage and two low-pressure turbine stages. Subsequently, GE developed the F110 design to offer a more powerful version, the F110-129. This produced 29,400lb of thrust, won business on the F-15E Strike Eagle and on Block 50 F-16Cs and F-16Ds and remains widely in service today, as does the F110-100.

The latest development by GE is the F110-132 powering the 80 Block 60 F-16s ordered by the United Arab Emirates (UAE). Employing a radial rather than a spray bar augmentor and incorporating durability improvements (including three one-piece 'blisks' to provide all three rotor stages in its fan module), the F110-132 produces 32,500lb of thrust and offers a service life of 4,300 TACs, even in the harsh desert environment of the UAE.

IMPROVING F110 RELIABILITY

Joe Guenther, general manager of GE Aviation's F101, F110 and F118 engines, also responsible for customer service for all military engines, said GE's next major development effort for the F110 programme was to improve its on-wing reliability further.

After initially increasing the F110-100 and F110-129 on-wing reliability to 4,000 TACs and 4,300 TACS respectively, GE began developing a Service Life Extension Program (SLEP) for the F110-129. This increased this engine's on-wing reliability to 6,000 TACs, effectively extending its time-on-wing between major overhauls from seven to ten years.

Guenther said that, using appropriate rights it owned as an equal partner with Snecma in CFM International, GE leveraged technology from the CFM56-7 – the world's most-common commercial turbofan engine – to provide a series of durability- and reliability-related upgrades for the F110-129 core. These included improvements in the 3-D aerodynamics of the F110-129's compressor airflow (to increase efficiency as well as rotor and structure life), adding cooling channels in the combustor (doubling its service life), making changes to aerodynamics, materials and cooling in its turbine blades and stages (increasing durability) and modifying the augmentor design (to increase durability, reduce maintenance and improve maintainability). The US government paid for qualification of the modification of the original

The GE Aviation F110-GE-132 turbofan engine rated at 32,500lb of thrust is used by the UAEAF Block 60 F-16E and F-16F fleet. GE Aviation

Crew chiefs assigned to the 555th Fighter Generation Squadron perform an engine run on an F-16 during an engine run certification at Aviano Air Base, Italy. USAF/Airman 1st Class Zachary Jakel

F110-129 design into the new F110-129 SLEP configuration.

According to Guenther, development of the SLEP core for the F110-129 turned a somewhat unique [F110] core into an identical bill of materials for any engine in the F101, F110-129 and F118 family. This commonality potentially allows the USAF to buy a SLEP upgrade kit and put it into any of those engines. GE produced SLEP kits for the F101 for installation in operational F101-102 engines in early 2016.

GE then fed the SLEP advances it developed for the F110-129 back into improving the CFM56-2 engines powering USAF C-135-family aircraft, as well as the US Navy's E-6B Mercury airborne command post jets as part of the CFM Propulsion Upgrade Program (C-PUP) involving CFM International and the USAF. Subsequently, GE self-funded development of a SLEP upgrade for the F110-100 to provide a 6,000-TAC interval between overhauls.

Guenther said some international customers expressed interest in the increased-life F110-100 SLEP modification for retrofit in their existing F-16s, including Greece, Israel and Turkey. He said GE's SLEP development effort for the F110-100 identified areas in the engine that couldn't be modified easily – mainly its low-pressure turbine module – and basically newly designed them, creating an engine which is very like the F110-129.

F110 COMPONENT IMPROVEMENT PROGRAMME

Separate from GE's SLEP development efforts was a continuing F110 Component Improvement Program (CIP), in which the USAF provided $30-35m to keep improving the engine's durability and reduce its maintenance and management workload.

GE drew upon its commercial-engine development work for F110 CIP inspiration, including work on new turbine and combustor designs to improve durability and reliability for operations in hot and harsh environments. From work on the GE90 and other large commercial engines, it learned that certain [blade] geometries and cooling schemes worked better than others.

One result was that the latest F110 turbine blades had very similar features to the latest GE90 turbine blades, even though they are much smaller. According to Guenther, GE also fed design-improvement experience from its commercial and F110 programmes back into CIPs for other engines, such as the T700, F404 and F414. Two other F110 CIP improvements are worth noting. One changed the design of the F110-129 fuel nozzle, which incorporated safety wire meant to lock it into position to make the design safer, but later proved to require more maintenance than the nozzle in the F110-100.

The change introduced a molar fitting that allowed locking of the F110-129 fuel nozzle into position but didn't require any safety wire, reducing the maintenance requirement. Also, GE's continuing engineering efforts to address operating capabilities in hot and harsh environments included modernising the F110-132's control system to provide full authority digital engine control, which the F110-129 already had. This addressed any potential F110-132 obsolescence issues.

F110 CONTRACTS

Senior leaders from the USAF, GE Aviation, StandardAero, the Defense Logistics Agency (Aviation) and Foreign Military Sales attended a ceremony at StandardAero's facility in San Antonio, Texas, on July 11, 2019, to celebrate the first GE F110-100 engine overhaul induction under the Pacer Pharaoh Program. The ceremony recognised the collaborative effort led by the USAF to upgrade the F-16 fleet of the Egyptian Air Force (EAF).

In May 2019, the Defense Logistics Agency (Aviation) and the USAF awarded a support contract to GE Aviation valued at more than $79 million for Engine Structural Integrity Program (ENSIP) repair and Service Life Extension Program (SLEP) upgrade of F110-100A and F110-100B engines to F110-100C standard.

The F110-100C SLEP upgraded the combustor, high pressure turbine, compressor and augmentor to extend the service life of the engine, a significant time-on-wing increase, a 25% improvement in cost per flight hour and a 50% extension in engine phase inspections.

A component of the Oklahoma Air Logistics Complex, the Propulsion Management Group (PMXG) had supported F110 engine upgrades during the previous decade. When PMXG faced issues with insufficient capacity, the USAF approached the DLA with support requirements to meet the needs of the EAF.

The Pacer Pharaoh Program support contract transferred the USAF's workload to GE Aviation, in collaboration with StandardAero, which enabled increased customer support at a competitive price. The collaboration was part of the USAF's Captains of Industry (COI) partnership, which used Supplier Capability Contracts (SCC) to streamline the procurement process to meet customer needs.

Chuck Darnell, head of the Propulsion Sustainment Division, Air Force Life Cycle Management Center, said: "EAF combat readiness and the USAF sustainment support for our international partner nations is key to the air force mission. To fly, fight and win with our partner nations is our goal."

It was the first F110 MRO relationship between GE and StandardAero and allowed GE to provide complete SLEP/ENSIP repair capability to their customers. StandardAero

An aerospace propulsion technician assigned to the 35th Maintenance Squadron, performs a test run of an F110 engine at Misawa Air Base, Japan. USAF/Airman Hannah Bench

Crew chiefs push an F110 engine into position for installation in an F-16 at Aviano Air Base, Italy. *USAF/Senior Airman Stan Parker*

provided engine level disassembly, reassembly and test portion of the work scope. GE provided engineering, material and the depot-level repair support at its facility in Winfield, Kansas. The agreement provided uninterrupted support for the EAF, reduced turn-around time and created new capabilities for GE Aviation.

In September 2019, GE Aviation's F110 family of engines surpassed 10 million flight hours. Backed by a continuous integration of new technology, F110 engines power almost 70% of the most advanced USAF F-16C and F-16D aircraft. Commenting on the milestone, Shawn Warren, VP and general manager of GE's Large Combat and Mobility Engines division, said: "The F110's cost-effective, high-performance operation, combined with its safety and reliability, increase mission capability rates and airmen readiness."

"Over the F110's lifetime, GE has continuously worked to maximise the engine's performance, minimise maintenance costs and increase its reliability and time on wing"

The first GE-powered F-16s entered service in 1987 and now power F-16 fleets in Bahrain, Bulgaria, Chile, Egypt, Greece, Israel, Oman, Slovakia, Taiwan, Turkey, the United Arab Emirates, and the USAF. As of March 2026, 3,800 F110 engines have been ordered worldwide in operation with 17 nations.

Over the F110's lifetime, GE has continuously worked to maximise the engine's performance, minimise maintenance costs and increase its reliability and time on wing. The newest F110 variants have gone through GE's Service Life Extension Program (SLEP), which includes three-dimensional aerodynamic technology derived from the CFM56 commercial engine family and upgrades to the combustor and high-pressure turbine. The enhancements generate up to a 25% improvement in cost-per-flying hour, a 50% increase in engine cycle life and a threefold increase in average time-on-wing. GE also provides engine overhaul support to the USAF through the Pacer Phantom programme, a contract mechanism for logistics or maintenance support provided by the company.

In April 2020, the Air Force Life Cycle Management Center (AFLCMC) awarded GE Aviation four contracts valued at $707m for F110-GE-129 engine production. The contracts fall under an existing indefinite-delivery/indefinite-quantity (IDIQ) contract to provide F110 engines, installs, spares and modernised engine management system computers for Block 70 F-16C and F-16D aircraft supplied under foreign military sales to Bulgaria, Slovakia, and Taiwan.

When GE Aviation celebrated 40 years of continuous production and improvement of the F110 engine at the Royal International Air Tattoo 2025, Sean Keith, executive product director for the F110 engine programmes at GE Aerospace, said: "We have been in continuous year-over-year production since 1984, and we are ramping production to meet strong market demand. In a somewhat unexpected turn, production levels for the F110 were expected to hit yearly levels not seen since 2009. The F110 has been updated significantly since it first reached the market. A full 92% of the parts have undergone some type of design change – whether it's new material, new coatings or an improved manufacturing or inspection process. The number one reason that our engine comes off wing is scheduled maintenance, the engine is designed so that 90% of all maintenance can be performed on-wing and at an on-site facility as opposed to a central depot.

"The F110 has even more latent capability that could be tapped into if needed, including thrust, range, and power extraction."

A cunning Marketing Ploy

An overview of Lockheed Martin's F-16 avionics upgrade.

A line of Republic of China Air Force F-16s configured to Viper upgrade standard assigned to the 4th Tactical Fighter Wing at Chiayi Air Base. Taiwan Ministry of National Defence

Starting this explanatory feature about the Viper upgrade it's appropriate to start with a few facts, which may surprise you. You can find the term 'F-16V' used in countless features posted on websites all over the internet in reference to advanced variants of the F-16.

However, it does not denote a variant of the jet, but the Viper avionics upgrade. The term is used by Lockheed Martin as a marketing indicator – like fifth-generation, another description for its F-22 and F-35 fighter aircraft. Any F-16A, F-16B, F-16C or F-16D fitted with the Viper upgrade retains its original production designation, so a Block 20 F-16A or F-16B with the Viper upgrade remains a Block 20 F-16A or F-16B. Lockheed Martin's marketeers opted to name the avionics upgrade Viper because the name has been used by F-16 pilots to refer to the aircraft for decades, even though its official name is the Fighting Falcon.

ORIGIN

The Viper upgrade started with a retrofit programme for the Republic of China Air Force comprising a package of systems centred around a new avionics suite, an AESA radar and operational flight program (OFP) software V1. Additional requirements from other customers led to follow-on configurations with V2 and V3 OFP software. Lockheed Martin made further improvements which were introduced on new build aircraft and are now offered in retrofit.

Mike McSpadden, Lockheed Martin's F-16 chief engineer, described the procedure as "a continual improvement process that builds on itself. Every time we gain a new F-16 customer, we add capabilities to the aircraft and, in most cases, those capabilities are retrofittable to older aircraft. We normally call the retrofit configuration the F-16 Viper upgrade, which is a package that includes an AESA radar, but there are other upgrades for the F-16 that don't include this. The F-16 Viper upgrade is different to a new-build Block 70, which has similar avionics but an airframe with a 12,000-hour service life and improvements to the airframe and some mechanical systems."

F-16 VIPER UPGRADE

The heart and soul of the Viper upgrade is a new state-of-the-art AESA radar. More specifically, the Northrop Grumman APG-83, a radar system that can conduct near simultaneous air-to-air and air-to-ground modes, which generates a lot of information for the pilot.

Discussing the upgrade, McSpadden said: "We had to upgrade the core computers to process the information. So we upgraded the mission computer, the display generator and the up-front control computer that provides up-front control for the pilot. Given the amount of information generated by the AESA radar and the sensors, we also incorporated a 6in x 8in high-definition centre pedestal display. To handle the amount of information and distribute it between new mission computers, sensors and displays, we installed a Gigabit Ethernet to supplement the legacy 1553 databus. Ethernet is like a communication superhighway.

"We undertook a lot of work to ensure the RF interface between the AESA radar and the electronic warfare systems were compatible. This was accomplished by integrating the new Viper Shield electronic warfare system. We also integrated an improved datalink and a new helmet mounted display."

These systems were part of the initial new-build Block 70 aircraft configuration, but further system improvements were introduced as Lockheed Martin gained more Block 70 customers. The company has already improved the Block 70 baseline OFP software which is offered in the Viper upgrade configuration. According to McSpadden: "It's like the second generation of the Viper upgrade. In production, we are in the process of implementing the new Common Digital Flight Control Computer 2, which has an advanced flight management system featuring an enhanced autopilot, auto throttle and deep stall recovery. These improvements were possible thanks to the greater memory and throughput to the flight control computer. Now we can offer that same upgrade in retrofit."

KEEPING PACE WITH THE USAF

Discussing the different phases of the Viper upgrade, McSpadden explained that each customer has a unique set of requirements: "A retrofit usually starts with a baseline configuration, so the kit we supply is tailored to the customer's baseline. For example, one customer wanted a new helmet-mounted display, which was subsequently integrated for a follow-on customer together with a new datalink. Configuration characteristics are unique to each customer, though the respective aircraft will look about the same."

As the largest operator of the F-16, how the USAF configures its aircraft tends to lead the configuration choices of FMS customers. For example, the F-16 Viper upgrade bought by numerous FMS customers has numerous similarities to the USAF F-16 upgrade. In fact, Lockheed Martin makes FMS F-16 configurations as common to the USAF F-16 configuration as possible, including those modified with the Viper upgrade.

The Defense Security Cooperation Agency states that major FMS programmes nurture long-term relationships with the US military, including access to joint training and doctrine and increased opportunities for interoperability with US forces.

"Lockheed Martin makes FMS F-16 configurations as common to the USAF F-16 configuration as possible, including those modified with the Viper upgrade"

USAF F-16s are being modified under a programme led by a team named the Post Block Integration Team (PoBIT). The team is part of the Air Force Life Cycle Management Center's Fighters and Advanced Aircraft Directorate. The USAF programme involves 608 Block 40 and Block 50 F-16s. Each one will undergo up to 22 modifications designed to improve lethality and ensure effectiveness for meeting current and future threats. Modifications include the APG-83 AESA radar, an upgraded mission computer to almost the same configuration as the Viper upgrade, a Link-16 datalink, cockpit modernisation, a high-speed databus, a new electronic warfare system, a new centre pedestal display, a programmable data generator and communication system upgrades. Installation of some modifications has already started and will continue over several years.

The programme involves six major commands, multiple bases, numerous companies and contracts totalling approximately $6.3 billion. A structural upgrade programme called the service life extension programme (SLEP) provides each USAF Block 40 and Block 50 F-16 aircraft with a 13,000-hour service life. McSpadden noted that the USAF upgrade programmes are designed to keep its F-16s flying until the 2045-2048, which also serves as a confidence-builder for FMS partners.

RETROFITS

To date, all Viper upgrade retrofits have been completed in the recipient customer nation using a kit shipped by Lockheed Martin. A kit comprises several packages which are installed on the aircraft in accordance with the work instruction card. Tools supplied with the kit are used to ensure components and parts are placed in the right location. Lockheed Martin also provides technical assistance.

Detailing the process, McSpadden said: "Some nations opt to undertake upgrades with the kits installed at its depot, Alternately, the air force can choose to nominate a company to undertake the work. In almost every instance, Lockheed Martin provides some kind of technical support to help overcome any issues with the installation.

"We normally undertake what we call a kit proof for the first two aircraft, usually an F-16A and an F-16B or an F-16C and an F-16D. We also have a lot of people on site to support the first kit installations. We also conduct a lot of training, so the air force or industry technicians understand how to read the plans and work instruction cards, where the parts go and how to use the tools. The technicians learn lessons and then start upgrading a second and third aircraft, performing more of the hands-on work themselves."

VIPER UPGRADE TEST PROGRAMME

Lockheed Martin designs an upgrade kit to meet the customer's requirements, which goes through a series of different system engineering design reviews. Handling quality simulator testing of the avionics package is conducted at Lockheed Martin's Fort Worth facility. Lockheed Martin modifies a flight test aircraft using either a production engineering specification or a flight test specification and loads the appropriate OFP software.

Once functional check flights are completed, the aircraft are flown to Edwards Air Force Base, California, for assignment to the 416th Flight Test Squadron. A component of the 412th Test Wing, the 416th is the Air Force Test Center's developmental test squadron for fighters. It tests all F-16s, USAF, FMS, new-build or upgraded for suitability of flying, maintenance and engineering. A test team assigned to the 416th creates the run cards that list the specifics of how a system will be assessed. During flight test missions, instrumentation installed on the aircraft collects data that is analysed by both Lockheed Martin and the USAF.

The F-16 Viper programme has remained active since the first two Republic of China Air Force (Taiwanese) aircraft arrived at Edwards in October 2015. The programme has tested jets from all FMS F-16 Viper upgrade customers, the first being Taiwan. The Republic of China Air Force is already operating the Viper upgrade configuration and continues to modify its remaining aircraft. In addition, Lockheed Martin completed further work on a couple of Taiwanese aircraft in preparation for a flight test programme of new capabilities.

The Hellenic Air Force Viper upgrade programme involved the modification of one aircraft at Fort Worth followed by flight testing by the 416th Flight Test Squadron at Edwards.

VIPER BASIC, VIPER PLUS

The first iteration of the upgrade was called Viper basic, followed by Viper plus, which features an advanced cockpit, stand-by flight instrument, changes to the centre pedestal display, electronic gauges, the new common digital flight control computer with autopilot and auto-throttle, a new helmet-mounted display and changes to some of the core computers. A Viper plus cockpit looks like the latest version of the Block 70.

Since the first Block 1 F-16s entered service with the USAF in 1978, those jets and each subsequent Block has operated with an M-series OFP software; M denotes mission computer. When Lockheed Martin introduced its Viper upgrade the baseline OFP was M6, the so-called launch standard for the Viper upgrade. The company changed is OFP designation nomenclature to the V-series. V1 and V2 were developed for retrofit programmes, as was V3, which recently went into production on the first Block 70 aircraft. Some aircraft retrofitted with V3 are in service. V4 is a production configuration still in development and will also be offered as a Viper upgrade. V4 runs the Common Digital Flight Control Computer 2, the advanced cockpit and provisions for a baseline IRST capability.

The Common Digital Flight Control Computer 2 is in development for the new-build Block 70. Similarly, the existing baseline IRST capability is being modified for Block 70 and Viper Shield will eventually be retrofitted to them. According to McSpadden, Lockheed Martin has future capabilities in work continuing its evolution in both retrofit and new production.

A few nations have signed agreements with the US government to implement the Viper upgrade to their respective fleets of F-16 aircraft, but Taiwan was the first F-16 operator in the world to field F-16s configured to Viper upgrade standard. Dubbed 'Feng Zhan', Taiwan embarked on a multi-year

The 30th Hellenic Air Force F-16 configured to Viper upgrade standard, an F-16D, was delivered back to the air force in January 2025. Hellenic Aerospace Industry

The Polish Ministry of National Defence signed a deal with the US to upgrade its 48 Block 52+ F-16 aircraft to Viper upgrade standard in August 2025.

$4.5 billion Viper upgrade programme for 140 F-16A and F-16B aircraft in early 2017. The last aircraft was handed back to the Republic of China Air Force in December 2025. Two ROCAF F-16s were upgraded by Lockheed Martin at its Fort Worth, Texas facility, which subsequently served as prototypes for Taiwan's Aerospace Industry Development Centre (AIDC), which undertook the remaining upgrades at its F-16 MRO hub in Taiwan. The ROCAF declared the 4th Tactical Fighter Wing based at Chiayi Air Base as operational with F-16s configured to Viper upgrade standard in November 2021.

In December 2018, Greece signed a $997m agreement with the US government for the upgrade of 84 Block 52, Block 52+, and Block 52 Advanced series F-16s to Viper upgrade standard. According to Lockheed Martin, the first two upgraded aircraft were delivered to the Hellenic Air Force in September 2022, the 30th aircraft was delivered back to the air force in January 2025, with all 84 scheduled to be complete by 2027. All work is being undertaken by Hellenic Aerospace Industry at its Tanagra facility.

In August 2025, the Polish Ministry of National Defence signed a deal with the US to upgrade its 48 Block 52+ F-16 aircraft to Viper upgrade standard. Lockheed Martin will serve as the primary contractor with the work undertaken at Military Aviation Works No. 2 in Bydgoszcz, which currently maintains C-130s and F-16s. The upgraded aircraft are planned to be returned to the Polish Air Force between 2030 and 2038.

The USAF F-16 upgrade programme involves 608 Block 40/42 and Block 50/52 aircraft. USAF/William R Lewis

VISTA Vision

An overview of the X-62A VISTA, a highly-modified F-16D used by the USAF Test Pilot School for the pursuit of artificial intelligence in military aviation.

Originally conceived as the NF-16D flying testbed and used by the USAF Test Pilot School (TPS) for flight testing of thrust vectoring, variable stability, advanced control laws and inflight simulation, the re-designated X-62A is now the foundation for the integration of artificial intelligence (AI), which the USAF cites as transformational to tactical and networked air combat. Between 1993 and 2021, the NF-16D Variable-stability In-flight Simulator Test Aircraft (VISTA) was operated by the TPS, a component of the 412th Test Wing based at Edwards Air Force Base, California, and maintained by Calspan until its redesignation in 2021.

In December 2025, the 412th Test Wing announced that the X-62 was undergoing a mission systems upgrade (MSU) to expand its role: "Building on DARPA's Air Combat Evolution programme – where the aircraft achieved a historic milestone by engaging in the first-ever human versus AI dogfight – the MSU will enable the X-62 to evaluate integration of combat systems

The X-62A VISTA in the skies above Edwards AFB, California. USAF/Richard Gonzales

and collaboration with airborne agents in increasingly complex environments. The upgrade will enable the X-62 to be fitted with an advanced radar and sensor(s) for employment in complex scenarios, and will evaluate the integration, collaboration and real-time decision-making capability of the aircraft's AI system."

Colonel Maryann Karlen, commandant of the Test Pilot School, explained: "As the air force expands its exploration of integrating autonomy into air and space operations, the X-62 is the bridge between the historical human-centred approach and tomorrow's integration of uncrewed combat aviation. The mission systems upgrade enables the X-62 to continue the journey in developing breakthroughs in AI and autonomy".

According to the 412th Test Wing, the X-62 will complement other Department of the Air Force investments in autonomy testing within operational environments, such as the ongoing Viper Experimentation and Next-Generation Operations Model (VENOM). The X-62 will support programmes that underpin the USAF's next-generation force structure, for example, advanced sensor operation and AI sensor data processing, air superiority demonstrations, autonomous collaborative platform capability and interoperability and resilience across advanced test ecosystems.

VISTA'S ORIGINS

The initial concept originated in the mid-1970s when the USAF recognised the need for a replacement for the NT-33A In-Flight Simulator (IFS) aircraft. Various design studies were conducted until the mid-1980s for the development of a full six-degrees-of-freedom in-flight simulator. The purpose was to develop a full IFS capability for small, fighter-type aircraft using an airframe that had performance characteristics representative of modern fighters. The studies resulted in the selection of the F-16 for a five-degrees-of-freedom IFS (pitch, roll, yaw, lift and thrust).

In-flight simulation is the process of augmenting a 'host' aircraft, in this case VISTA, through a control system to simulate the handling characteristics and dynamics of another aircraft. Since the flight control system of the simulated aircraft is implemented in the host platform, its characteristics can be assessed in a real-world environment. Specific flight control system changes, flying qualities, architectures, failure modes, gain changes and control systems can all be evaluated.

Production of the VISTA NF-16D was given to General Dynamics, Fort Worth Division, Texas, in 1988 (now Lockheed Martin Aeronautics). Calspan Aerospace was selected to develop and integrate the aircraft's Variable Stability System (VSS) because of the company's expertise in flight control system development and IFS. The N prefix given to the VISTA denoted its status as special test, permanent whose configuration is drastically changed that returning the aircraft to its original configuration or conversion to standard operational configuration is beyond practicable or economic limits.

CONFIGURATION

The resulting VISTA aircraft was a mixture of many different features, most of which were already available from previous F-16 production programmes. VISTA is a Block 30 F-16D, serial number 86-0048, airframe in Peace Marble II configuration, including a large dorsal fairing for installation of additional electronic equipment.

The aircraft is fitted with a General Electric F110-GE-100B engine (with provisions for a thrust vectoring nozzle) and heavyweight landing gear due to the weight of the additional equipment. Internally, VISTA is configured as a Block 40 F-16 with associated avionics and Digital Flight Control Computer (DFLCC), a wide field of view head-up display (HUD) and an APG-68 radar. Nine external store stations are available for tanks, pods and weapons, with a programmable digital interface to each station. The standard F-16 weapons

The NF-16D VISTA shown in its original paint scheme and fitted with a spin chute used when a test pilot cannot recover from a stall or spin using normal flight controls. USAF

system was changed to a foreign military sale (FMS) configuration, meaning the AIM-120 AMRAAMs and nuclear weapon capabilities, chaff/flare dispenser, radar warning receiver, the gun and its associated equipment were removed.

The fully programmable HUD, multi-function displays (MFDs), avionics and remaining F-16 systems enable the VISTA to be used for current and future weapons flight research experiments. The aircraft is also capable of boom/receptacle and probe/drogue aerial refuelling using an SFI 370-gallon ART/S tank pod, dry hook-up only.

Additional modifications made to the VISTA include an upgraded hydraulic system with larger pumps and lines, removal of hydraulic flow restrictors from the control surface actuators to meet increased control surface slew rate requirements and a larger electrical generator.

OPERATIONAL USE

VISTA became operational in January 1995 after delivery to Calspan's Flight Research Facility in Buffalo, New York, where it was maintained and operated under a co-operative research and development agreement with the Air Force Research Laboratory (AFRL) at Wright-Patterson Air Force Base, Ohio. In October 2000, the USAF Test Pilot School enhanced its flying qualities and test management programme curriculum by integrating the VISTA, with the aircraft permanently transferred to Edwards.

VISTA programmes to date have included IFS, flight control development and risk reduction of the F-22, India's Light Combat Aircraft, Lockheed Martin's JSF X-35 Concept Demonstration Aircraft and the X-38 Crew Recovery Vehicle. It has been involved in numerous test management programmes into flight control system research. Evaluations included Have Filter (for a new design for a software rate-limiting algorithm), Have Cap (for power approach flying qualities), Have Track (for aerial refuelling flying qualities) and Have Panic, to support the AFRL's quest for remotely piloted aircraft advanced flight control laws. During Have Panic tests, various flight control laws embedded in the aircraft's unique Variable Stability System were evaluated. This project brought TPS one step closer to making VISTA the world's first fully reconfigurable manned, surrogate remotely piloted aircraft.

The VISTA team also worked with the 416th Flight Test Squadron (FLTS) at Edwards on the Auto Air Collision Avoidance System (ACAS) under Have Posit II. Members of TPS' Class 12B completed proof of concept and risk reduction testing on the Auto ACAS systems developed by Lockheed Martin in response to a 2003 memorandum issued by Secretary of Defense Donald Rumsfeld to

Roger Tanner and Bill Gray flew the NF-16D Variable Stability In-Flight Simulator Test Aircraft from Hill Air Force Base, Utah, to Edwards on January 30, 2019. USAF/Christian Turner

The then NF-16D VISTA in formation with a KC-135 tanker during a mission from Edwards Air Force Base, California. USAF

"The resulting VISTA aircraft was a mixture of many different features, most of which were already available from previous F-16 production programmes"

reduce the frequency of aircraft mishaps by 50% – a target later increased to 75%. Have Posit II tested Auto ACAS operation during pre-planned engagement scenarios that required activation of an avoidance manoeuvre and evaluated the system during advanced rejoins and formation flight, with aggressive manoeuvres performed to replicate the highly dynamic environment of air combat training.

The NF-16D VISTA was modified with P5 combat training system pods that housed the Auto ACAS algorithm for testing. The algorithm used a logical sequence of steps to determine whether a potential threat had been detected. Once the threat of an air-to-air collision had been established, the software selected one of nine automatic avoidance manoeuvres.

Auto ACAS increases the range between the aircraft by directing one of the following manoeuvres: maintain what it is doing, bunt, straight pull or increase bank in either direction, then pull up to 5G. The Have Posit II testing was the first time that the this algorithm took control of the aircraft and physically manoeuvred it away from an airborne collision. At the time, Captain Joshua Hall, project manager for Have Posit II, said: "What we were focusing on was making sure the aircraft automatically manoeuvred and that the manoeuvre was accurate. So we had one aircraft always maintaining its position, then we had VISTA coming in to demonstrate that the algorithm was functioning properly as it performed automatic avoidance manoeuvres."

The team successfully completed five missions and performed 29 automatic avoidance manoeuvres, demonstrating Auto ACAS was fully capable of avoiding an air-to-air collision threat. Each test point provided the team with a valid piece of data

NF-16D VISTA 86-048 undergoes pre-flight checks on the flight line at Hill Air Force Base, Utah, on January 30, 2019. USAF/Alex Lloyd

that was used to ready Auto ACAS for initial testing.

Conducting an evaluation of Auto ACAS was a priority for both the Air Force Research Laboratory and Lockheed Martin, as the software promised to reduce the number of air-to-air collisions without impeding mission performance. The Have Posit II test team took vital steps to help the AFRL and Lockheed Martin Aeronautics refine leading-edge sense and avoid technology.The team made recommendations thath were evaluated and incorporated into larger flight testing by the 416th Flight Test Squadron in early 2014 and entered service with the USAF later that year.

VARIABLE STABILITY SYSTEM

Prior to its redesignation, the VISTA's primary sub-system for in-flight testing was the Variable Stability System (VSS), a digital and analogue system that interfaced with existing F-16 avionics and sensors. The main benefit of the VSS computers was the ability to be rapidly reprogrammed, making the VISTA ideal for rapid prototyping and quick turnarounds of desired system changes. The controls and displays for the pilot-in-command or safety pilot were in the aft crew station. The safety pilot controlled the VSS configuration through the multi-function displays (MFDs) and the control panel. The evaluation pilot, in the forward crew station, had programmable variable feel centre stick and side stick controllers and displays. Either controller could be engaged using the select switches on the feel engage/VSS status panel. For operations not requiring an evaluation pilot, the forward crew station could serve as an operator or observer station with complete interface capabilities through the VSS.

The variable feel system was digitally controllable and fully programmable, providing a wide range of controller characteristics – such as simulated aircraft dynamics and variable feel controller characteristics – that could be selected during flight from a group of

"When a safety trip occurred, the VSS disengaged and control of the VISTA was returned to the safety pilot"

stored configurations. Specific characteristics could be changed individually using the VSS Configuration Control System (CCS) menus. When the VSS was engaged, the front crew station occupant could have direct control capability to the aircraft using the centre stick or side stick controls and rudder pedals. Trim buttons or an autonomous control system could also be programmed to control the aircraft.

If the throttle servo was engaged, the evaluation pilot also controlled aircraft throttle inputs. They flew the aircraft through the VSS control laws with full authority of the control surfaces. The VSS control laws included the augmentation to modify the F-16's basic stability and control characteristics to mimic the simulated aircraft's basic dynamics, as well as the simulated aircraft's control law wrapped around the un-augmented model.

Both manual and automatic safety trips are included in VISTA. Automatic safety trips would disengage the VSS to provide protection against exceeding the simulation operating envelope and/or overstressing the airframe. When a safety trip occurred, the VSS disengaged and control of the VISTA was returned to the safety pilot. The safety pilot can fly the VISTA using standard F-16 controls and either pilot had the ability at any time to manually disengage the VSS and return control to the safety pilot with normal F-16 flight controls. A mode could also be selected at any time enabling the evaluation pilot to fly the normal F-16 control laws while the safety pilot could be involved with other tasks.

The VSS included aircraft feedback signals from various sources onboard. The aircraft linear and angular acceleration signals are determined from three sets of dual redundant three-axis accelerometers. Aircraft attitude, inertial position and inertial velocity are obtained from the standard Block 40 F-16 ring laser gyro inertial platform. Angle-of-attack (AoA) and angle-of-sideslip (AoS) are

Flying high over the Californian desert near Edwards Air Force Base, NF-16D VISTA 86-048 during a flight during the Multi-Axis Thrust-Vectoring programme. USAF

determined from signals generated by the left and right AoA probes and the upper and lower AoS probes on the nose of the F-16.

Information is provided by the standard F-16 air data system. APG-68 radar signals (air-to-air and air-to-ground) are also available. In 2014, VISTA was modified to install a high bandwidth, line-of-sight datalink enabling it to be flown as a remotely piloted aircraft (RPA) or be controlled fully autonomously from a ground station. The entire RPA operation (aircraft dynamics, guidance, navigation, flight controls, ground stations, communication links, etc) couldn be simulated in a real-world environment without risking an actual test article.

Thomas Hill, senior test pilot of the Curriculum Standards Branch at the USAF Test Pilot School, elaborated on the value VISTA brings to the school: "The VISTA is the centrepiece of our technical assets at the Test Pilot School. As a variable stability aircraft, VISTA provides us the opportunity to conduct curriculum training and experimental research that would be prohibitively expensive or simply too risky using other less capable platforms. The student educational experience is enhanced as they solidify theoretical concepts learned in ground-based academics through hands-on training only allowed by the flexible architecture built into VISTA."

X-62A REDESIGNATION

On June 14, 2021, the NF-16D VISTA was redesignated as the X-62A to reflect an upgrade programme designed to support USAF autonomy testing. At this time, William Gray, chief test pilot at VISTA and TPS, said: "The VISTA aircraft has given almost 1,000 students and staff members the opportunity to practice testing aircraft with dangerously poor flying qualities, and to execute risk-reduction flight test programmes for advanced technologies."

The VISTA underwent an upgrade to replace the VSS with a new system called the System for Autonomous Control of Simulation (SACS) at the time of the redesignation, The new system was integrated to support the Air Force Research Laboratory's autonomy-focused Skyborg programme.

Skyborg sought to enable the USAF to operate and sustain low-cost, teamed aircraft that could thwart adversaries with quick, decisive actions in contested environments. It's aim was to enable airborne combat mass by building a transferable autonomy foundation for a family of layered, unmanned air vehicles.

The AFRL is prototyping a suite of autonomy and unmanned system technologies equipped with capabilities that can support a range of USAF missions. Skyborg is not seeking to replace human pilots, but rather provide them with key data to support rapid, informed decisions. If successfully proven, Skyborg would endow manned aircraft with greater situational awareness and survivability during combat missions.

The Skyborg team conducted an 190-minute flight test with the Skyborg autonomy core system (ACS) aboard a Kratos UTAP-22 tactical unmanned vehicle at Tyndall Air Force Base, Florida, on April 29, 2021.

NF-16D VISTA 86-048 taxies at Hill Air Force Base, Utah, on January 30, 2019, for its ferry flight back to Edwards AFB following depot level maintenance, modifications and a new paint scheme. USAF/Alex Lloyd

Dubbed milestone 1 of the Autonomous Attritable Aircraft Experimentation (AAAx) campaign, the ACS demonstrated basic aviation capabilities and responded to navigational commands, while reacting to geo-fences, adhering to aircraft flight envelopes and demonstrating co-ordinated manoeuvring. It was monitored from both airborne and ground command and control stations.

Milestone 1 was the first step in testing the ACS and started a sequence of experimentation events planned over several months. It marked the first time an active autonomy capability was demonstrated on an air force test range. Follow-on events demonstrated direct manned and unmanned teaming between aircraft and multiple ACS-controlled unmanned airframes.

The aim of the Skyborg Vanguard programme was to integrate full-mission autonomy with low-cost, attritable unmanned air vehicle technology to enable manned-unmanned teaming. Skyborg provided the foundation on which the USAF could build an airborne autonomous 'best of breed' system of systems that adapts, orients and decides at machine speed for a wide variety of increasingly complex mission sets. William Gray said: "We found ways to use VISTA that were not envisioned by the original designers, so we ran into frustrating limitations. The modifications addressed these limitations and profoundly improved our ability to test an almost unlimited variety of radical control law configurations quickly and safely. Even so, the X-62A will continue to serve as a [TPS] curriculum aircraft."

The X designation denotes aircraft that are designed for testing configurations of a radical nature and are not normally intended for use as tactical aircraft. The X-62A VISTA serves as a main asset of the TPS research division and is currently the only active X plane supporting a test pilot school curriculum."

AI

AI algorithms developed under DARPA's Air Combat Evolution (ACE) programme and loaded on the X-62A VISTA were used to control the aircraft in flight during a series of test flights lasting more than 17 hours in December 2022. The test flights flown from Edwards Air Force Base, California, were the first with AI engaged on a tactical aircraft.

Detailing the flight test programme, Lieutenant Colonel Ryan Hefron, DARPA programme manager for ACE, said: "We conducted multiple take-offs and landings with numerous test points performed on

A USAF Test Pilot School mission from Edwards. Note the In-Flight Simulator marking on the air inlet. USAF

The VISTA aircraft in formation with F-16D 85-572/ED assigned to the 416th Flight Test Squadron based at Edwards on April 30, 2019, prior to its arrival back at the Californian super base. USAF/Richard Gonzales

each sortie to put the algorithms through varying starting conditions, against various simulated adversaries and with simulated weapons capabilities. We didn't run into any major issues, but we did encounter some differences compared to simulation-based results, which is to be expected when transitioning from virtual to live. This highlighted the importance of not only flight testing the advanced autonomous capabilities, but doing so on testbeds like VISTA, which allowed us to rapidly learn lessons and iterate at a much faster rate than with other air vehicles. VISTA allowed us to streamline the programme by skipping the planned subscale phase and proceed directly to full-scale implementation, saving a year or more and providing performance feedback under real flight conditions.

Explaining the X-62's application to AI testing, Dr Christopher Cotting, director of research at the USAF Test Pilot School, said: "VISTA will allow us to parallelise the development and test of cutting-edge AI techniques with new uncrewed vehicle designs. This approach, combined with focused testing on new vehicle systems as they are produced, will rapidly mature autonomy for uncrewed platforms and allow us to deliver tactically relevant capability to the combat air forces."

Recent upgrades implemented by the USAF include an updated VISTA Simulation System (VSS) provided by Calspan, and Lockheed Martin's Model Following Algorithm (MFA) and System for Autonomous Control of the Simulation (SACS). The integrated SACS and MFA systems provide new capabilities so the VISTA can be used to conduct advanced flight test experiments featuring autonomy and AI. The new mission system with VSS, MFA and SACS enable autonomous aircraft algorithm development and integration to be advanced. At the heart of the SACS system is the Enterprise-wide Open Systems Architecture (E-OSA) which powers the Enterprise Mission Computer Version 2 (EMC2) dubbed the Einstein Box. Lockheed Martin's Skunk Works developed the open systems architecture.

Additional components of SACS include integration of advanced sensors, a multi-level security system and a set of Getac tablet displays in both crew stations to enhance VISTA's capabilities and maintain its rapid-prototyping capability. This configuration allows software changes to be made quickly to increase the frequency of test flights and speed the pace of AI and autonomy development for urgent national security needs.

One such sensor destined for the X-62 is Raytheon's PhantomStrike strike active electronically scanned array (AESA) radar. Raytheon describes this as a low-cost, lightweight multi-function radar designed for smaller fighters and uncrewed tactical aircraft. The air-cooled radar weighs 150lb, has highly-efficient gallium nitride (GaN) antennas with improved power and range over existing gallium arsenide radars. The PhantomStrike radar will form an essential part of the X-62's role in developing AI software for future autonomous combat jets.

DARPA'S ACE

DARPA's Air Combat Evolution (DACE) programme was staged to increase trust in combat autonomy by using human/machine collaboration within visual range engagements as its challenge problem. DACE applied existing AI technologies to within-visual-range engagement during experiments of increasing realism, while using methods to measure, calibrate, increase and predict human trust in combat autonomy performance. It also scaled the application into more complex scenarios that involved multiple aircraft in simulated operational scenarios with live data feeds, in preparation for subsequent campaign-level experimentation.

> **"The X designation denotes aircraft that are designed for testing configurations of a radical nature and are not normally intended for use as tactical aircraft"**

DARPA has developed a military strategy dubbed mosaic warfare that uses a large, disaggregated and heterogeneous mix of low-cost, smart sensors and weapons rather than a few exquisite, monolithic platforms." Mosaic warfare is designed to overwhelm an enemy with complexity, speed and agility by connecting multiple drones and systems, known as tiles, into a flexible, resilient and adaptive network.

DARPA stated that: "In a future air domain contested by adversaries, a single human pilot could increase lethality by effectively orchestrating multiple autonomous unmanned platforms from within a manned aircraft. This shifts the human role from single platform operator to mission commander. DACE aims to deliver a capability that enables a pilot to attend to a broader, more global air command mission while their aircraft and teamed unmanned systems are engaged in individual tactics.

"DACE uses a hierarchical autonomy framework in which higher-level cognitive functions (eg, developing an overall engagement strategy, selecting and prioritising targets, determining best weapon or effect) may be performed by a human, while lower-level functions (ie, details of aircraft manoeuvres and engagement tactics) is left to the autonomous system. For this to be possible, the pilot must be able to trust the autonomy to conduct complex combat behaviours in scenarios such as the within-visual-range engagement before progressing to beyond-visual-range engagements.

"The DACE demonstrations were designed to bridge the gap between simple current physics-based automated systems to complex systems capable of effective autonomy within highly dynamic and uncertain environments at mission speeds.

Technologies used in the DACE programme address four primary challenges: to increase air combat autonomy performance

The VISTA aircraft has six markings applied: VISTA (top of the vertical stabiliser), X-62 (vertical stabiliser), Calspan Aerospace (base of vertical stabiliser), USAF Test Pilot School (fuselage spine), DARPA and AFRL (fuselage aft of canopy), and In-Flight Simulator (air inlet). Its striking paint scheme reflects its one-of-a-kind experimentation role. USAF/Richard Gonzales

in local behaviours (individual aircraft and team tactical), to build and calibrate trust in air combat local behaviours, to scale performance and trust to global behaviours (heterogeneous multi-aircraft) and to build infrastructure for full-scale air combat experimentation.

WORLD FIRST

In September 2023, the Edwards AFB was the location for an aerial engagement between two F-16s like no other: one aircraft was controlled by AI and one by a pilot. A joint team, comprising USAF, DARPA and contractor personnel claimed the feat to be a world first.

Colonel James Valpiani, the DARPA programme manager in the Tactical Technology Office and chief of combat autonomy at the Air Force Test Center, said: "The potential for machine learning in aviation, whether military or civil, is enormous. How do we do it, how do we do it safely and how we train them are the questions that we are trying to answer."

A series of trials were staged involving the AI-controlled X-62A VISTA with a pilot onboard and a standard manned F-16D in-visual-range combat scenarios. The two aircraft conducted defensive and offensive manoeuvres, flying at up to 1,200mph. At one point, they were only 2,000ft apart, turning inside of each other. Pilots on board the X-62 had controls to deactivate the AI system if necessary, but DARPA claimed the pilots never needed to utilise the safety switch.

Taking off from Edwards AFB, the X-62A flew 21 missions under the control of four different AI algorithms during fighter manoeuvres, totalling 17 hours of flight time. The series of tests was the first-time machine learning had been used to operate a fighter jet. The aircraft's AI algorithms analysed data and made real-time judgments. DARPA believes that engaging in a battle between an AI powered plane and a human is a transformational point in the history of aerospace. DARPA officials emphasised AI's capability to a bigger end: demonstration that AI could be trusted to fly a fighter jet, paving the way to even greater airborne autonomy testing.

But Colonel Valpiani highlighted the lack of a pathway to achieve flight certification for an aircraft controlled by machine learning, but expects autonomous capabilities derived from programmes like DACE to augment but not necessarily replace human functions. And on the questions of AI supplanting human pilots, he said: "Speculative, almost philosophical – better left for air force planners who decide on policy. We think that there's tremendous promise in the way we have approached this and the lessons that we're learning."

On May 3, 2024, US Secretary of the Air Force Frank Kendall flew in the X-62. Commenting on the flight, John Clark, VP and general manager of Lockheed Martin Skunk Works, said: "The need for innovation at speed and scale is greater than ever. The X-62A VISTA is a crucial platform in our efforts to develop, test and integrate AI, as well as to establish AI certification standards that will revolutionise the future of aerospace. Our proven hardware and software architecture enables safe and controlled environments for AI agents and advanced algorithms to rapidly prototype and develop."

This photo of the forward fuselage of the VISTA aircraft clearly shows details of the current paint scheme. USAF/Richard Gonzales

The first six former Royal Danish Air Force F-16s in formation over the South Atlantic en route to Río Cuarto-Cordoba Air Base on December 6, 2025.
Fuerza Aérea Argentina

Nation 31

In December 2025, Argentina received its first six F-16s from Denmark, making it the 31st nation to operate the F-16.

Argentina's acquisition of former Royal Danish Air Force F-16s began in late March 2024, when Danish Minister of Defence, Troels Lund Poulsen, arrived in Buenos Aries to work through an agreement between the two countries for the purchase of 24 aircraft. A letter of intent for the purchase worth $300 million was signed by Poulsen and Argentina's Minister of Defence, Luis Petri. The deal involved US financing for just short of $700 million over a six-year term, covering the cost of the aircraft, a spares package, munitions, simulators and training. In a media release, Poulsen said: "The decision to sell the Danish jets to Argentina has been carried out in close collaboration with the American government, which has approved the sale of the US produced aircraft."

In Royal Danish Air Force service, the aircraft were configured with the Terma Electronic Combat Integrated Pylon System and Pylon Integrated Dispenser Station, a modified weapons pylon housing a missile approach warning system (MAWS), a radio frequency (RF) jammer and chaff/flare dispensers. The pylons are carried on stations 3 and 7.

Given the UK's military embargo on Argentina following the 1982 Falklands conflict, Petri discussed the F-16 contract with British Ambassador to Argentina, Kirsty Hayes, in Buenos Aries before the contract was signed on March 25. The sale and transfer of the Danish F-16s was conducted under the Foreign Military Sales programme and managed by the US Defense Security Cooperation Agency. Denmark's Ministry of Defence Acquisition and Logistics Organisation is handling the transfer of the aircraft and simulators in co-ordination with the US government, and the procurement process is being supervised by Argentina's military logistics directorate. Deliveries will be completed by 2028 and the aircraft will be based at Tandil, home of the VI Air Brigade and Grupo Aerea 6 de Caza, with maintenance undertaken at Río Cuarto.

The $300 million deal was signed by Poulsen and Petri during a ceremony at Skrydstrup Air Base in Denmark on April 16, 2024. Poulsen commented: "I am very pleased that the Danish F-16 aircraft, which have served us well over the years and have been thoroughly maintained and upgraded, [will] now be used in the Argentine Air Force. With the deal, we are strengthening Danish-Argentinian defence co-operation, while Argentina will become part of the global F-16 family."

On July 2, 2025, Danish defence company Terma announced it had signed a support agreement with the Argentinian Ministry of Defense and the Argentine Air Force, to provide key upgrades and support services related to the F-16's electronic warfare systems, as part of an aircraft refurbishment led by Lockheed Martin Aeronautics. Terma's agreement includes delivering software and hardware enhancements, mission planning tools, ground support equipment and engineering assistance.

In a media release, Henriette Hallberg Thygesen, CEO and President of Terma, said: "This agreement reflects Terma's core strength in delivering mission-critical systems and integrated solutions across platforms and domains. We combine deep technical expertise with decades of operational experience to support our partners in meeting complex defence requirements."

F-16A M-1020 makes a spirited fly-by at Río Cuarto-Cordoba Air Base.
Fuerza Aérea Argentina/Cabo Primero Ari Detomasi and Cabo Lautaro Vera

Two Fuerza Aérea Argentina F-16s turn and burn at Río Cuarto-Cordoba Air Base. Fuerza Aérea Argentina/Cabo Primero Ari Detomasi and Cabo Lautaro Vera

Five of the former Royal Danish Air Force F-16s arrive at Río Cuarto-Cordoba Air Base on December 6, 2025. Fuerza Aérea Argentina/Cabo Primero Ari Detomasi and Cabo Lautaro Vera

The first six former Royal Danish Air Force F-16s landed at Río Cuarto-Cordoba Air Base on December 6, 2025. The other 18 aircraft will be delivered in batches of six in December 2026, 2027 and 2028. On the funding side of the deal, the US government provided $40 million in financing as the down payment on the $560 million Foreign Military Sales package, which includes training, maintenance and long-term support also provided by the US: the remaining near $140 million is being funded by Argentina.

The USAF announced on March 10, 2025, that it had awarded Lockheed Martin Aeronautics an un-definitised contract worth up to $265.96 million as part of an FMS deal with Argentina which includes updating the F-16 Operational Flight Program software. According to a Department of Defense notice, Lockheed will conduct the work in Fort Worth, Texas, Denmark and Argentina, with an expected completion date of March 31, 2032. Funding of $53.2 million was obligated to Argentina at the time the contract was awarded.

On January 21, 2026, the Argentine Air Force posted a notice on social media regarding its F-16 fleet: "As part of the preparation process to begin flight activities in the near future, containers loaded with tools, spare parts, components and armament intended to sustain future F-16 operations have arrived in country and our pilots continue to conduct simulator activities and ground training."

Argentine Air Force F-16A M-1009 landing at Río Cuarto-Cordoba Air Base. Fuerza Aérea Argentina

On December 6, 2025, Argentina's President Javier Milei welcomed the first six F-16s purchased from Denmark.

F-16B M-1005 lands at Río Cuarto-Cordoba Air Base. Fuerza Aérea Argentina/Cabo Primero Ari Detomasi and Cabo Lautaro Vera

F-16A M-1009 parked on the flight line at Río Cuarto-Cordoba Air Base. Fuerza Aérea Argentina/Cabo Primero Ari Detomasi and Cabo Lautaro Vera

Protecting

Freedom

In operation since August 2024, Ukraine's F-16 fleet has reportedly shot down more than 2,000 Russian drones and missiles.

A Ukrainian Air Force F-16A loaded with four AIM-9 Sidewinder missiles and two Terma modified pylons with chaff/flare dispensers and a missile warning system. *Ukrainian Air Force Command*

In a video released on YouTube by the Ukrainian Air Force in early January, a senior pilot qualified on the F-16 gave insight to the aircraft's service introduction with the Ukrainian Air Force. The pilot reflected on the difficult conditions encountered by the initial cadres of pilots sent to train on the F-16, who had to learn different rules and procedures in double-quick time, familiarise themselves with a new fighter jet and its systems and overcome the challenge of learning from instructors who only spoke English: "It was very exhausting, to be honest. But we had a goal, we understood that they were waiting for us at home, that the enemy was shelling our cities, killing our people, capturing our territory. So, we gritted our teeth to the last and continued."

After completing their training, the pilots realised the tactics that had been given to them were not entirely suited to the Ukrainian theatre: "We had to come up with tactics for how we would destroy cruise missiles and strike drones, and how we would fight the enemy near the line of contact."

The commitment of the pilots to learn how to fly and operate the F-16 is borne out by some general statistics. Less than a month after the first F-16 was in country, the Ukrainian pilots were ready to fly combat sorties against aerial targets in August 2024 and, by the beginning of 2026, the F-16 squadron had shot down more than 1,000 targets, mostly Shahed long-range one-way attack drones, jet-powered drones and cruise missiles, as well as over 1,600 ground targets.

The pilot said that virtually every F-16 sortie flown includes enemy missiles being launched at the Ukrainian jets: "The game is still very, very tough in the air and very, very risky. If you're not aware of the launch of a missile, you're dead."

"US President Joe Biden announced that the United States would support training of Ukrainian pilots on the F-16s."

Opposite: A Ukrainian Air Force F-16A loaded with two AIM-9 Sidewinder, two CATM-120 AMRAAM captive air training missiles, and two Terma modified pylons with chaff/flare dispensers and a missile warning system. *Ukrainian Air Force Command*

Below: A Royal Danish Air Force F-16A and an F-16B fly alongside a KC-135 Stratotanker after aerial refuelling. *US Air National Guard/SSgt Kenneth Shaner Brown*

He cited the MiG-31 *Foxhound*, Su-35 *Flanker* and the Su-57 *Felon* fighters as being the biggest threat to the F-16s: "They have the ability to be in the combat zone, at high altitudes, waiting for our groups to strike. Unfortunately, we do not have such an opportunity."

To counter the threat of enemy missiles, the F-16s are forced to fly lower: "We also must use manoeuvre tactics when enemy aircraft come at us, lock us up and launch air-to-air missiles at our planes. But regardless of this, with these limited capabilities, we carry out the task. We know that we are taking a risk. When we strike targets on the ground, we understand that the guys are sitting in the trenches – it's hard for them there and they need our help. Aviation must support them, so this is one of the main tasks for us."

The pilot said he and his colleagues especially like the F-16's targeting system, adding that partner air arms who helped train him and other pilots are learning from the Ukrainian experience and adjusting their tactics, particularly those used to defend cities and critical infrastructure against relentless enemy cruise missile and drone strikes.

The pilot thanked the partners who are supporting the Ukrainian military, especially in providing F-16 aircraft, and called upon them to not slow down, asserting "We can do more."

UKRAINE'S F-16 JOURNEY

On February 8, 2023, Volodymyr Zelensky made a historic address to members of the Houses of Commons and the Lords at Westminster Hall in London. Zelensky presented Lindsay Hoyle, the Commons speaker, with a fighter pilot's helmet with a handwritten request: "We have freedom, give us wings to protect it." Subtle but direct, Zelensky was asking the UK and NATO for fighter aircraft – F-16s, F-18s, Gripens,

"The game is still very, very tough in the air and very, very risky. If you're not aware of the launch of a missile, you're dead."

Mirages, Rafales or Typhoons – any type to help the Ukrainian Air Force fight off and strike Russian forces in occupied territory.

Until mid-May, Zelensky's requests for F-16 fighter aircraft were rebuffed, but US President Joe Biden announced that the United States would support training of Ukrainian pilots on the F-16s. This paved the way for Ukraine to take delivery of the fighter. Speaking to reporters in Washington DC on May 22, 2023, USAF Secretary Frank Kendall said: "F-16s will give the Ukrainians an increment of capability that they don't have right now, but the aircraft are not going to be a dramatic game-changer,

A Royal Norwegian Air Force F-16A aircraft flies behind a USAF KC-135 Stratotanker. US Air Force/Airman 1st Class Luke Milano

A Royal Norwegian Air Force detachment at Skyrdstrup Air Base, Denmark, provides instructor support on F-16s for Ukraine's air defence. Norwegian Ministry of Defence

WHICH TYPE OF F-16?

Since the first F-16s were rolled off the then General Dynamics production line in Fort Worth, Texas in 1979, more than 4,600 aircraft have been built. Over 130 aircraft remain on order with Lockheed Martin and will be produced at its Greenville, South Carolina, plant.

As detailed above, Denmark, Norway and the Netherlands are donating F-16s that were built in the early Block 10 and 15 lots. All the aircraft destined for Ukraine are configured in the Mid-Life Upgrade (MLU) standard, which underwent an upgrade in the 1990s. Generally designated F-16AMs and F-16BMs, the M denoting MLU, the aircraft are equipped with multiple systems ranging from sensors to self-protection which enable them to conduct day and night operations in all weather conditions. Some information provided by the Belgian Air Component explains how they are configured:

Modular mission computer *At the heart of the F-16 weapon system is a modular mission computer (MMC) that supports the integration and use of sensors and weapons and provides an improved pilot-vehicle interface. The MMC is 42% less bulky, 55% lighter and uses 37% less electrical power.*

APG-66 radar *The APG-66(V2) fire control radar, equipped with a new signal data processor, enables a track-while-scan mode for up to ten targets as well as a six-on-six AIM-120 capability. The APG-66(V2) provides a 25% improvement in detection and tracking range, an enhanced Doppler beam sharpening mode and enhanced air-to-ground and ground mapping modes.*

Advanced IFF An F-16AM is equipped with an APX-113 advanced identification friend-or-foe (AIFF) system which is fed by the upper interrogator fuselage mounted antenna array mounted on the upper forward fuselage in front of the canopy. The AIFF systems enables the delivery of AIM-120 AMRAAM missiles to ranges beyond the missile radar's limits.

AAQ-33 Sniper targeting pod
Carried on a hard point on the right-hand side of the air inlet, the Sniper pod features a geo-stabilised camera that remains focused on the same point on Earth, despite the high speed and altitude of the aircraft. It functions in day and night conditions, feeding imagery to a cockpit screen watched by the pilots, who can control the camera using the side stick controller. The pod features a laser designator and can generate still images of target areas. Images of Ukrainian F-16s fitted with AAQ-33 Sniper advanced targeting pods confirm the system's acquisition by Kyiv. Sniper's service introduction was reportedly made concurrently with the AGR-20 laser-guided rocket, dubbed the Advanced Precision Kill Weapon System II.

Link-16 The Link-16 network enables an F-16 pilot to share information efficiently and to maintain a maximum overview of the entire airspace, where other aircraft are located, how much armament and fuel remain on board, and which enemy targets they have detected and are striking.

Joint helmet-mounted cueing system
The helmet component of the JHMCS projects information on the pilot's visor, removing the need to look down into the cockpit for information. Systems such as the radar, camera and missiles are slaved to the pilot's head movements such that sensors can be aimed very quickly in the direction of a potential target in the air or on the ground.

Night-vision goggles NVGs are a device used by a pilot for night-time operations. The device comprises a pair of binoculars that amplify the remaining light and generates an image in different shades of green to enable vision in darkness.

Electronic warfare An F-16AM is equipped with a suite of systems that detect and warn the pilot. A radar warning receiver (RWR) alerts the pilot when his aircraft has been detected by an enemy radar system, while visual and audio signals indicate where the hostile radar system is located. An electronic jammer, carried externally on the aircraft, disrupts the enemy radar's system to continue following the aircraft. A missile warning system (MWS) consists of sensors that can detect an approaching infrared-guided missile. Visual and audio signals in the cockpit alert the pilot and flares are released to deceive the missile and redirect it away from the aircraft. Images released of Ukrainian Air Force F-16s show the aircraft loaded with a Terma modified pylon with chaff/flare dispensers and missile warning system integrated to the aircraft's internal self-protection suite.

Air-to-air weapons
An F-16AM is armed with two types of air-to-air missiles: the AIM-120 advanced medium-range air-to-air missile (AMRAAM) and the AIM-9 Sidewinder infrared-guided missile. The AMRAAM is initially fired at a target and guided by the aircraft's radar. Guidance is then assumed by a mini-radar housed in the missile's nose, which enables the pilot to turn away from the hostile aircraft and remain outside of enemy engagement zones. An AIM-9 is equipped with an infrared seeker that detects and guides the missile to heat sources from an enemy aircraft. An AIM-9 is extremely effective for close range air-to-air combat given its manoeuvrability and cueing provided by the JHMCS. Weapons loads seen in imagery of Ukrainian F-16s include live AIM-9L and AIM-9M Sidewinders with either four or six missiles carried. The F-16 is also equipped with an M61A1 20mm cannon that can be used against aerial and ground targets. It carries 511 rounds and can fire at a rate of 100 per second.

Air-to-surface munitions
An F-16AM can carry a variety of laser- and GPS-guided air-to-surface munitions, the most common of which are the GBU-12 laser-guided bomb and the GPS-guided GBU-31 and GBU-38 joint direct attack munitions. When employing the GBU-12, the pilot identifies the objective using a targeting pod and illuminates or spikes the target with a laser. The weapon flies towards the reflected laser energy. Laser-guided weapons can only be used in relatively good weather conditions because the pilot must be able to see his target to use the laser effectively. When employing the GBU-31 or GBU-38, the pilot loads the co-ordinates of the target into the weapon before releasing it. Based on GPS signals, the weapon knows the exact position of the target, adjusts on its trajectory and is re-programmable in terms of its trajectory angle, direction and speed.

as far as I'm concerned, for their total military capabilities."

Secretary of Defense Lloyd Austin had already received requests from countries who wanted US permission to train Ukrainians on the F-16. Operators of F-16s must seek permission from the US government before aircraft can be transferred to another nation, in accordance with the terms of a foreign military sales agreement. In August 2023, the US government assured Denmark and the Netherlands that the approval of transfer requests for F-16s to go to Ukraine when the pilots were trained would be expedited.

Six Ukrainian pilots and dozens of maintainers started training on the F-16 at Skyrdstrup Air Base, Denmark, in late August 2023. An additional six joined the programme, with some completing a basic

Ukrainian Air Force Command

A Ukrainian Air Force F-16A loaded with two AIM-9 Sidewinders and two AIM-120 AMRAAMs breaks away from a second aircraft. Ukrainian Air Force Command

programme of training with the RAF in the UK, which stated: "The group comprised six experienced Ukrainian combat fighter pilots who received aviation-specific English language training to increase their ability to engage with coalition training and support. A further ten Ukrainian trainee pilots took part in the language training and remained in the UK to continue with practical basic flight training."

On January 3, 2024, the Norwegian Ministry of Defence (MOD) announced it would provide two F-16BM aircraft and ten instructors from the Royal Norwegian Air Force to support training of UkrAF personnel in Denmark.

Norway's fleet of F-16s was formally retired on January 6, 2022, and replaced with the F-35A Lightning II. Oslo subsequently sold 32 former Royal Norwegian Air Force F-16s to Romania. When Norway joined the multinational F-16 training coalition for Ukraine in July 2023, it began returning some of its then-retired aircraft to operational status just for this purpose, ultimately pledging to donate an unspecified quantity of its retired F-16s to Ukraine on August 24.

On January 5, 2024, the two F-16BMs – one of which was serial '689' – were transferred from Bodø Air Base, Norway, to Skrydstrup to join the training efforts. Some of the ten Royal Norwegian Air Force instructors had been in Denmark to support UkrAF pilot training since October 2023. On January 4, Belgium also announced its intention to back the Danish training efforts by lending two of its F-16BM aircraft and some 50 training personnel from March until September 2024.

On August 20, 2023, the US gave approval for the transfer of F-16s to Ukraine from the European nations after months of lobbying by Kyiv. Denmark and the Netherlands became the first two countries to pledge to donate their outgoing F-16 fleets to the Ukraine at the NATO summit held at Vilnius in Lithuania in July 2023. Copenhagen is replacing its F-16s with 27 F-35As and 19 of its outgoing F-16s will be donated to Ukraine. Subsequently, Norway and Belgium also promised to donate F-16s, raising the total to at least 79 aircraft that are expected to be supplied to Ukraine. Up to 20 were planned to be delivered by the end of 2024, with the rest handed over in 2025.

On August 24, 2023, while speaking at a Pentagon press call, US Air Force Brigadier General Pat Ryder, the Pentagon's press secretary, confirmed that Ukrainian pilot training was expected to begin in October at Morris Air National Guard Base in Tucson, with Arizona Air National Guard's 162nd Wing. Ryder said: "The training provided by the United States will complement the F-16 pilot and maintenance training that's already underway in Europe and further deepens our support of the F-16 training coalition led by Denmark and the Netherlands. By making this announcement, the US is pre-empting any training capacity constraints in Denmark and the Netherlands' training pipeline to ensure the aircraft are fielded to Ukraine as quickly as possible. Ukraine will ultimately determine the number of pilots that will require training."

Two Royal Netherlands Air Force F-16As take-off for a mission from Leeuwarden Air Base. Royal Netherlands Air Force

An F-16A, a former Royal Danish Air Force aircraft, takes off from an undisclosed location in Ukraine. Ukrainian Air Force Command

On November 7, 2023, the Netherlands delivered the first five of 18 F-16s to Feteşti Air Base, Romania, home of the European F-16 Training Centre, which was inaugurated on November 13. Fetesti is home to Baza 86 Aeriana and Escadrille 53, currently the only Romanian Air Force F-16 squadron. It is equipped with 17 former Portuguese Air Force aircraft. The training at the Romanian facility is run by Lockheed Martin and subcontractors, Daedalus Aviation Group, Draken International, GFD, a subsidiary of Airbus Defence and Space and ILIAS Solutions for the Romanian Air Force, as well as other NATO countries and Ukraine. The usual three-year process of qualifying a combat pilot on the F-16 has been compressed to just nine months for the Ukrainian airmen.

On January 3, 2024, the Norwegian government announced it had delivered two F-16s and sent ten instructors to Skyrdstrup Air Base in Denmark for the training programme. Norway also donated more F-16s to Ukraine, joined by Belgium, Denmark and the Netherlands. Denmark has pledged 19 and the Netherlands 24, including six aircraft earmarked for sale to US adversary provider Draken International. In early February, the Dutch government scrapped the Draken deal. The six F-16 aircraft will now be delivered to Ukraine.

By early February, four Ukrainian pilots were undergoing F-16 training at Morris Air National Guard Base in Tucson, with 20 maintainers undertaking English-language training at Joint Base San Antonio, Texas. Speaking at a press conference on January 23, 2024, Celeste Wallander, assistant secretary of defense for international security affairs at the Pentagon, said: "We are aiming to provide an initial operating capability for Ukraine with its F-16 programme in 2024, which would entail trained pilots, the platforms, trained maintainers and sustainers, infrastructure and spare parts and ammunition."

NATO countries that have supplied equipment to Ukraine have displayed a reluctance for it be used to hit targets within

Afterburner power generated by the Pratt & Whitney F100-PW-220 turbofan engine makes light of getting this Ukrainian Air Force F-16 airborne. Ukrainian Air Force Command

An F-16A with Ukraine's national insignia on its tail parked on a dispersal at an undisclosed location with a standard AMRAAM-Sidewinder load-out. Ukrainian Air Force Command

> **"Ukrainian F-16s have intercepted around 2,000 drones and missiles since entering combat operations."**

Russia itself, for fear of broadening the conflict beyond the borders of Ukraine. Russian reaction to the delivery of the F-16s has been predictable, mainly concerning anti-NATO rhetoric as well as repeating threats that any country hosting Ukrainian fighters is "a legitimate target." On July 31, 2024, Kremlin spokesperson Dmitry Peskov stated their arrival would not change the course of the war. However, he also said that rewards have been offered to Russian servicemen who shoot down an F-16.

On August 4, 2024, Zelensky confirmed that the first batch of F-16s had arrived in Ukraine (reportedly being delivered in late July), during an event held at an unidentified Ukrainian Air Force base. August 4 is Air Force Day in Ukraine, with Zelensky describing the arrival of the former NATO aircraft as the start of "a new chapter" for the service: "I am proud of our guys who are mastering these jets and have already started using them for our country." He went on to "thank all the partners who are really helping with the F-16 and the first countries that accepted our request for aircraft: Denmark, the Netherlands, the United States."

On the night of September 16, six former Royal Netherlands Air Force F-16s reportedly landed at Minsk Mazowiecki, Poland's easternmost military air base, located less than 100 miles from the border with Ukraine, where they were handed over to the UkrAF. The event was not officially confirmed.

On September 26, 2024, the US announced it would train 18 UkrAF pilots in 2025, and acknowledged the transfer of an undisclosed number of AGM-154 joint stand-off weapons to Ukraine for use on its F-16s.

Ukraine has received F-16s from Denmark, the Netherlands and Norway. But what about Belgium? The nation first promised to donate F-16 aircraft to Ukraine in July 2023, signing a security and long-term support agreement with Ukraine on May 28, 2024, yet no aircraft hade been transferred from the Belgian Air Force to Ukraine, with delivery timelines repeatedly postponed. According to Belgium's Ministry of Defence the primary reason are the delays to deliveries of F-35A aircraft, the type chosen by the Belgian government to replace its fleet of F-16s in 2018. Without enough F-35s delivered, the Belgian Air Force must continue to meet its operational needs with its fleet of F-16s, which are expected to be retired by the end of 2028. The pace of pilot training and a consequent lack of pilots was also cited by unnamed Ukrainian officials as a second reason for the delays ofo F-16 transfers.

In early March, reports in the *Kyiv Post* suggested that Ukrainian Air Force F-16s ran short of US-made AIM-9 Sidewinder air-to-air missiles from late November to mid-December 2025 after supplies from partners temporarily dried up.

According to the newspaper: "During the shortage, Ukrainian pilots conducted daytime sorties and attempted to shoot down drones using the F-16's cannon, one source said. Night operations were considered too dangerous because Russian drone attacks typically occur after dark. Pilots also attempted to reuse missiles that had failed to fire during earlier missions after maintenance, occasionally succeeding."

The air-to-air missile shortage ended in December when partner countries supplied Ukraine with additional AIM-9s and, according to one source cited by Reuters, Ukrainian F-16s have intercepted around 2,000 drones and missiles since entering combat operations.

Peninsula Operations

Overview of a Republic of Korea Air Force F-16 squadron at Seosan AB.

Seosan Air Base is home to the Republic of Korea Air Force's (RoKAF) 20th Fighter Wing, equipped with KF-16s assigned to four flying squadrons. The wing constantly trains to counter any form of aggression from the Democratic People's Republic of Korea (North Korea) so it is ready to immediately enter a fight if necessary.

All fighter pilots go through the RoKAF's training pipeline, starting with the elementary phase flying the KAI KT-100, followed by a nine-month basic phase on the KAI KT-1 Woongbi turboprop, culminating with the nine-month advanced phase flying the KAI T-50 Golden Eagle. Pilots then enter combat readiness training (CRT) comprising 50 hours of flight time with the F-16 operational conversion unit at Seosan.

OPERATIONAL TRAINING

After completing F-16 CRT, pilots are posted to a tactical squadron where they receive specialised weapon qualification training with handling AGM-84 Harpoon and AGM-88 HARM missiles. Each training programme includes academics, simulator rides and flying.

All RoKAF F-16 squadrons are multi-role capable and tasked with air-to-air, air-to-ground, close air support, suppression of enemy air defences, and maritime strike roles. Each squadron follows a daily flight schedule based on the taskings set by the fighter wing and its training requirements. According to one squadron commander who spoke on condition of anonymity: "We can generate up to 25 sorties in a flying day, but while the ongoing KF-16 upgrade programme is underway, the daily total has decreased slightly. Air-to-ground and air-to-air training are conducted simultaneously on the same sortie.

"Due to the environment of facing North Korea, we try to maintain the minimum defensive posture, so we are always conducting all roles. We perform lots of air-to-air and air-to-ground missions, including close air support which is conducted in conjunction with the USAF to support JTACs and TACPs from the Republic of Korea Army and US Forces Korea.

"We must maintain a minimum qualification standard for employing the AGM-88 HARM in the suppression of enemy air defence role and the AGM-84 Harpoon for maritime strike. For example, a pilot must fly a HARM mission at least once every three months and a Harpoon mission once every six months. Our flight schedule is arranged to accommodate all such training requirements."

HIGH-END TRAINING

The RoKAF regularly deploys its tactical fighter squadrons to Eielson Air Force Base to participate in Exercise Red Flag-Alaska. For safety reasons, the RoKAF opts to only deploy two-seat aircraft to America's 49th state for participation in exercises like Red Flag and has done so since it first participated in the exercise back in 2013. Flight time and the associated fatigue faced by the pilots are the primary concerns. According to the squadron commander, in the future, the RoKAF expects to ferry single-seat KF-16s to Alaska.

In 2022, the RoKAF deployed three single-seat KF-16s to Australia for Exercise Pitch Black, an option made possible by a stop in the Philippines and consequently fewer safety issues.

A deployment to Eielson made in June 2023 involved the first combined tanker operation using a RoKAF KC-330 and USAF KC-10s. At the time, the RoKAF KC-330 had an operational employment limitation in place. Consequently, the KC-330 was limited to conducting just two of the eight aerial refuellings required. These were conducted between Korea and Japan. The remaining six aerial refuellings were conducted with USAF KC-10s.

During a typical Red Flag deployment at Eielson, RoKAF KF-16s start flight operations with live weapons employment on the Joint Pacific Alaska Range Complex as part of Exercise Distant Frontier. Opportunities to drop inert and live weapons are few and far

Republic of Korea Air Force KF-16Ds fly over the 77,000 square mile Joint Pacific Alaska Range Complex during Red Flag-Alaska in June 2023. USAF/SSgt Jessi Roth

A KF-16C takes off from Seosan Air Base, Republic of Korea, during a buddy wing exercise between RoKAF and USAF fighter squadrons. USAF/Senior Airman Taylor Curry

KF-16 UPGRADE

On November 21, 2016, Lockheed Martin announced a $1.2 billion contract under the US Foreign Military Sales programme to retrofit all 134 of the RoKAF's Block 50 and Block 52 KF-16s with its Viper avionics upgrade. A KF-16C or KF-16D fitted with the upgrade retains its original production designation, but uses the RoKAF designations KF-16CU and KF-16DU.

The heart and soul of the Viper upgrade is a new state-of-the-art AESA radar. More specifically, the Northrop Grumman APG-83, a radar system that can conduct near simultaneous scans in air-to-air and air-to-ground modes, which generates a lot of information for the pilot.

Discussing the upgrade, a Lockheed Martin spokesperson said: "We had to upgrade the core computers to process the information. So we upgraded the mission computer [MC 7000AH modular mission computer], the display generator and the computer which provides upfront control for the pilot. Given the amount of information generated by the AESA radar and the aircraft's other sensors, we also incorporated a 6in x 8in high-definition centre pedestal display. To handle the amount of information and distribute it between new mission computers, sensors and displays, we installed a gigabit-rated ethernet to supplement the legacy 1553 databus. Ethernet is like a communication superhighway. We undertook a lot of work to ensure the RF interface between the AESA radar and the electronic warfare systems were compatible. This was accomplished by integrating the new Viper Shield electronic warfare system. We alsovadded an improved datalink and a new helmet mounted display."

The first iteration of the Viper upgrade was called Viper Basic. This standard was followed by Viper Plus which features an advanced cockpit, a stand-by flight instrument, changes to the centre pedestal display, electronic gauges, a new common digital flight control computer with autopilot and auto-throttle, a new helmet-mounted display and changes to some of the core computers.

When Lockheed Martin introduced its Viper upgrade the baseline Operational Flight Program (OFP) software was M6, the so-called launch standard. The company changed its OFP designation nomenclature to the V-series. V1 and V2 were developed for retrofit programmes.

Commenting on the KF-16 upgrade, the squadron commander said: "An upgraded KF-16 has two notable capabilities. It provides the pilot with greater situational awareness and better weapon employment."

AGM-84K HARPOON

The AGM-84K Harpoon stand-off land attack missile – extended range (SLAM–ER) is a high sub-sonic, long-range, network-enabled weapon system designed to provide day, night and adverse weather precision strike capability against moving and stationary land and maritime targets. SLAM-ER can employ numerous operating modes. It measures 172in in length, 13.5in diameter and has an 86in wingspan. It weighs 1,450lb and carries a 500lb warhead

A Korean Block 52 KF-16D breaks away from a KC-135 tanker after an aerial refuelling. USAF/Senior Airman Matthew Seefeldt

between in the RoK so the ability to do so in the Alaska environment from a different base is welcome.

Red Flag starts immediately after Distant Frontier. For RoKAF KF-16 pilots trained in multi-role operations, the daily mission tasking is dependent on the requirements and objectives set by the mission commander. The squadron commander told the author: "Everything can change for us during the mission. For example, we can conduct escort air-to-air and then suddenly switch to protecting the package. We can swap roles; we can conduct the defensive counter air mission, get an aerial refuelling, and then change to close air support. It depends on the requirements of the mission commander for the mission of the day.

A Republic of Korea KF-16D uploads fuel from a KC-135R Stratotanker assigned to the 909th Air Refueling Squadron based at Kadena Air Base, Japan. USAF/SSgt Jessi Roth

In advance of the exercise all the main rules of the missions are agreed, but the details of each player and the timeline can be changed by the mission commander. As per the agreement with the USAF reached prior to the exercise, one RoKAF KF-16 pilot served as the mission commander for one Red Flag mission. Each squadron participating in the exercise provides a mission commander for at least one mission. The commander's team launched each of its six KF-16s for every mission, split between a two-ship flying with the Red Air force and a four-ship with the Blue Air force.

The squadron commander commented: "The technical function and capability of a KF-16D is the same as a KF-16C. However, the ability to fly two pilots on every mission enables each pilot to gain experience of a Red Flag exercise, situational awareness is increased and pilots get opportunities to improve their communication skills. During

GBU-31 JDAM

The GBU-31 joint direct attack munition (JDAM) is a guidance set that converts an unguided free-fall 2,000lb bomb into an accurate, adverse weather smart armament. The guidance set consists of a tail kit containing INS and GPS, a set of aerosurfaces and an umbilical cover. A JDAM can be launched from very low to very high altitudes in a dive, toss and loft or in straight and level flight. It measures 150in in length and 25in diameter, weighs 2,000lb and carries a 945lb warhead.

A Republic of Korea Air Force crew chief helps a KF-16 pilot into his cockpit prior to a Red Flag-Alaska mission at Eielson Air Force Base, Alaska. *Mark Ayton*

AGM-88 HARM

The AGM-88 high-speed anti-radiation missile (HARM) is a supersonic air-to-surface missile designed to seek and destroy enemy radar-equipped air defence systems. The missile consists of four sections: guidance, warhead, control and the rocket motor. It measures 164in in length and 10in diameter, weighs 800lb and carries an 140lb warhead.

missions flown back home in the RoK, the main role for the pilot in the aft seat is to monitor the systems and the mission execution."

Comparing Red Flag-Alaska to high-end training in the ROK, the squadron commander said: "We have an exercise called Korea Flying Training (KFT) held twice in the first half of the year, followed by further drills in the second half. These are staged under the Vigilant series. KFT is a joint employment exercise with the USAF that simulates a fight against North Korea. The size and objectives of KFT is much the same as Red Flag-Alaska. KFT focuses on North Korea as the virtual enemy, Red Flag-Alaska also focuses on a virtual enemy, but one that is not North Korean. Not only is Red Flag-Alaska a new experience for our pilots, it's also highly beneficial."

AIRSPACE AND BUFFER ZONES

KF-16 crews based at Seosan use various areas of airspace, some close to the base and others further afield. The squadron commander explained: "The closest airspace we use is within three minutes flying time after take-off. We fly at altitudes up to 40,000ft, though we can climb above 40,000, but we don't tend to train at that altitude."

On January 8, 2024, South Korea's Joint Chiefs of Staff officially declared that the buffer zones outlined in the September 2018 inter-Korean military agreement are no longer in place. In the announcement, the Joint Chiefs said: "North Korea declared the nullification of the September 18 inter-Korean military agreement last year [November 2023] and recently held three consecutive days of live artillery exercises near the western maritime border, which is supposed to be a no-hostility zone. Their behaviour demonstrates that the no-hostility zone no longer exists."

Under the September 2018 agreement, buffer zones were established over land, air and sea to prevent unintended military skirmishes in border regions between North and South Korea from escalating into war. On November 22, South Korea announced the suspension of its commitment to the no-fly zone outlined in the September 2018 pact following an announcement by North Korea that it had successfully launched its third military surveillance satellite. In response, North Korea announced it was scrapping the September 2018 agreement on November 23.

Prior to the nullification of the buffer zones, RoKAF and USAF aircraft were restricted to fly within airspace close to the Demilitarised Zone (DMZ) between North and South Korea, designated the purple zone, and were not permitted to fly across a no-fly line. These restrictions would only be lifted in the event of a contingency operation or potential conflict with North Korea.

Republic of Korea Air Force KF-16D 92-046 on take-off from Eielson Air Force Base. *Mark Ayton*

A Republic of Korea Air Force KF-16D on a mission for a Red Flag-Alaska exercise. *USAF/SSgt Joshua Turner*

The tip of Portugal's spear

Josef Campion reports from Base Aérea 5 Monte Real, home to the Portuguese Air Force's two F-16 Fighting Falcon squadrons.

Located in Portugal's central region, the town of Monte Real is host to the Força Aerea Portuguesa (FAP; Portuguese Air Force) Base Aérea 5 (5th Air Base), home station to two fighter squadrons equipped with F-16s: Esquadra 201 'Falcões' (Falcons) and Esquadra 301 'Jaguares'.

Esquadra 201 transitioned to the LTV A-7P Corsair II attack aircraft in 1980, an aircraft which was occasionally employed in the air-to-air role due to a lack of dedicated fighter aircraft. That gap was finally filled by F-16s supplied to Portugal under the US Foreign Military Sales programme dubbed Peace Atlantis. The first delivery took place in 1994, comprising Block 15 aircraft configured to operational capability upgrade (OCU) standard.

Sister squadron Esquadra 301 began operations in January 1969 at Aeródromo Base 5 Nacala, Mozambique, operating the Fiat G-91 with the Esquadra 502 numberplate, condicting anti-guerrilla, interdiction and attack missions, with three permanent detachments established at Porto Amélia, Mueda and Nampula, in addition to other non-permanent detachments at Nova Freixo, Vila Cabral and Base Aerea 10 Beira. At the end of the war and the restructuring of FAP, the squadron began operating from Base Aérea 6, Montijo, under the designation Esquadra 62. In 1978, the unit was re-designated Esquadra 301 and continued to operate the Fiat G-91 until 1993 for close air support, battlefield interdiction and tactical aerial reconnaissance.

In 1994, Esquadra 301 moved to Base Aérea 11 Beja,and re-equipped with the Alpha Jet, maintaining the same assigned mission set. Several reconnaissance pods and electronic warfare (EW) systems could be fitted on the back seats of the cockpit dubbed R2-D2, due to their similarity with the *Star Wars* droid. The EW capability proved effective and provided 301's jets with an effective self-defence capability.

Esquadra 301 conducted its last flight with the Alpha Jet in November 2005, followed by its transfer to Base Aérea 5 Monte Real, where it became the first Portuguese F-16 MLU frontline all-weather, day and night, air defence and conventional attack squadron.

FAP F-16S

The first batch of 20 Block 15 OCU F-16s – 17 F-16As and three F-16Bs – were delivered to Portugal in 1994 and remained in service until 2011. Sixteen of the F-16As (one was lost in 2002) were upgraded to F-16AM standard under the MLU programme. Eleven were completed by November 2010 and the sixteenth example was redelivered by September 2012. All three F-16Bs were upgraded to MLU standard between 2011-2013.

A second batch of 25 former USAF Block 15 aircraft arrived in 1999, under the Peace Atlantis II programme, comprising 21 F-16As and four F-16Bs. The Portuguese government decided to upgrade its fleet under the MLU programme as the original OCU standard aircraft were outdated. Nineteen of the 21 F-16As delivered under Peace Atlantic II underwent MLU and the remaining two were used as a source of spares. It was 2003 when the first F-16 (MLU) made its maiden flight and finally entered service in November 2005 with Esquadra 301.

FAP F-16s carry a variety of armaments including AIM-9 Sidewinder and AIM-120 AMRAAM air-to-air missiles, Mk82 and Mk84 general purpose bombs, GBU-12 laser-guided bombs, GBU-31 JDAM (GPS-guided), and

A Portuguese Air Force F-16AM clearly showing all four blade antennas of the IFF system just forward of the cockpit canopy, and an AAQ-28 Litening targeting pod. USAF/TSgt Emili Koonce

A Portuguese F-16AM flies behind a USAF KC-135 over the west coast of Greece during Exercise Ramstein Flag 24 on October 4, 2024. USAF/TSgt Emili Koonce

GBU-49 (dual-mode) precision-guided munitions, with target information generated by a Litening 4 targeting pod.

The F-16 remains Portugal's primary frontline aircraft, executing defensive and offensive counter air-to-air and air-to-ground (air interdiction, close air support and anti-surface warfare) roles.

F-16 TRAINING

After completing either fast jet conversion training or an introduction to fighter fundamentals course with Air Education and Training Command, new FAP pilots selected for the F-16 undertake three curriculums to qualify as combat-ready. First up is the basic course (BC) to qualify the pilot to fly in visual and instrument meteorological conditions, IFR and VFR. Next is initial qualification training (IQT) to teach the pilot about the F-16's sensors and armaments, as well as tactics to employ the aircraft for basic and planned missions. Finally, the initial mission qualification training (IMQT) course involves the pilot flying complex mission scenarios that F-16s could be tasked with and requires application of the tactics learned in the IQT phase. All pilots must successfully complete all three courses.

Most students' responsibilities remain the same during the air-to-ground and air-to-air missions. To qualify as a combat-ready wingman (WG), new pilots must be able to conduct a safe flight, comply with their cockpit tasks while maintaining situational awareness of the missionand constantly fulfil their responsibilities with their flight lead by remaining in adequate visual formation, using their sensors and employing weapons when required to do so. Specific missions are flown that require sufficient knowledge of the aircraft, its systems, weapons and tactics to be used. Once a pilot is declared combat-ready, they must complete a pre-requisite minimum number of air-to-air and air-to-ground missions on an annual basis.

WARTIME ROLE

On October 13, 1998, NATO issued the activation order for Operation Determined Force to pressure the Yugoslav authorities to comply with the ceasefire in Kosovo. However, with the escalation of events, Operation Allied Force began on March 24, 1999. This was the most intensive military operation in Europe since the end of World War Two, representing the first time that NATO had successfully employed (almost exclusively) air power to coerce the adversary's leader to change his behaviour. The Kosovo War – which was almost exclusively aerial – prolonged the bombing of Yugoslavia for 78 days until, on June 10, 1999, President Slobodan Miloševic agreed to sign a peace plan and the withdrawal of Yugoslav forces from Kosovo began.

On January 21, 1999, three F-16As from Esquadra 201 landed in Aviano, supported by 60 military, remaining under operational control of the Alliance, to be employed in defensive counter air missions (CAPs) and the escorting of high-value assets (E-3A AWACS and KC-135 or KC-10 aerial refuelling aircraft).

The national detachment, designated Pilgrim Falcon, lasted until June 26 and was supported by three C-130Hs. During the 157 days of deployment, 285 sorties were made, totalling 1,057.5 flight hours.

Due to the complexity of Operation Allied Force missions, the average flight time was four hours and 35 minutes – the longest flight was seven hours and 15 minutes, with four aerial refuellings.

Both Esquadra 201 and 301 hold the same responsibilities, which include offensive counter-air (OCA) to destroy, disrupt or degrade adversary air and missile capabilities. Ideally, most OCA operations will prevent the launch of aircraft and missiles by destroying them and their supporting infrastructure and systems on the ground. Another role is defensive counter-air (DCA), which involves active and passive air operations to detect, identify, intercept and destroy adversary air and attacking missiles or to reduce the effectiveness of such attacks should they escape destruction; 40% of the FAP F-16 continuation training programme is dedicated to OCA and DCA.

Air interdiction involves operations to divert, disrupt, delay, degrade or destroy an adversary's military potential before it can be brought to bear effectively. Each air interdiction mission starts with a commander's intent analysis, followed by a thorough target study, an extensive review of the rules of engagement, intelligence updates, threat examinations and an inventory of the capabilities available. One pilot dubbed the flight lead is responsible for organising the flight brief which all aircrews must attend.

Close air support (CAS) is conducted against hostile targets that are located near to friendly ground forces. Conducting CAS requires detailed integration of all aircrew and JTACs to avoid friendly-fire incidents. They may or may not require complex preparation before the flight – some requests are for immediate response due to the urgent nature of the support required by the ground troops involved. In such a scenario the communications and

F-16AM 15103 with tail markings for the 60th anniversary of Esquadra 201 'Falcões'. The aircraft is loaded with an ALQ-131 electronic countermeasures pod on the port side hard point on the air inlet. USAF/TSgt Emili Koonce

F-16AM 15132 taxis in at Base Aérea 5 Monte Real, Portugal during an edition of Exercise Real Thaw, an annual exercise to develop interoperability for contingency operations between Portugal and NATO allies. USAF/SSgt Nathanael Callon

understanding between pilots and JTACs are crucial for mission success.

Anti-surface warfare missions are flown in support of broader counter-maritime operations with the objective of destroying or neutralising adversary naval surface forces using the same munitions that are used for conventional air-to-ground attacks.

QUICK REACTION ALERT

The FAP maintains two-armed F-16 aircraft on standby in dedicated hardened aircraft shelters (HAS) at Monte Real around the clock, 365 days per year, for quick reaction alert (QRA) missions. Personnel are on shift for 24 hours, with a readiness state of 15 minutes, which means aircraft must be airborne within that time from when the launch bell rings.

Tango (training) scrambles keep QRA pilots current on the correct procedures to get the aircraft airborne within this time. Once airborne, pilots run through various practice intercepts with national controllers to validate procedures as well as correct execution on all sides. Such an event can be conducted with aircraft that agree to be intercepted for training or between F-16s assigned to the two FAP squadrons. At any point during the training sortie, the jets can be re-tasked to a real-life scramble mission.

BALTIC AIR POLICING

Since 2007, the FAP has participated in NATO air policing missions in the Baltic region, within the framework of NATO's Assurance Measures, as well as operations in Iceland, Romania and Poland. During its 2023 deployment to Lithuania, the FAP F-16 detachment completed 480 flight hours and identified 50 aircraft belonging to the Russian Federation.

In 2024, FAP once again deployed to Siauliai Air Base, Lithuania, with four F-16s between April and July. The BAP mission covered the airspace of Estonia, Latvia and Lithuania, with the identification and interception of aircraft that were not in compliance with international aviation rules or that posed a potential risk to air traffic and public safety.

During a ceremony held at Monte Real Air Base on March 21, the Chief of the General Staff of the Armed Forces, General José Nunes da Fonseca, said: "The BAP mission has a preponderant persuasive purpose, a sign of the Alliance's collective determination to dissuade the Russian Federation from any aggression or threats against NATO countries. The Portuguese military will carry out important and essential tasks, in accordance with Portugal's commitment to the collective defence of NATO."

During the BAP detachment in May 2025, FAP F-16s participated in Exercise Neptune Strike, a joint training event that also involved Czech Air Force helicopters and Lithuanian special operations forces. Staged as a series of exercises, Neptune Strike is designed to demonstrate NATO's ability to integrate high-end maritime strike capabilities, strengthen deterrence, and ensure freedom of navigation across critical waterways. It also aims to secure strategic maritime chokepoints while testing interoperability across air, land and sea. The air component is designed to strengthen air security in the Baltic region through the practice of standardised combat tactics, techniques, tactics and procedures.

F-16AM 15112 configured with three external fuel tanks launches in full afterburner from Base Aérea 5 Monte Real enroute to Iceland. Josef Campion

During its time at Siauliai Air Base, FAP also participated in other exercises. One example was Baltic Connection 24 (BALTCON24), an air defence exercise that took place between July 7-19, designed to integrate NATO forces in air defence operations with centralised command and control. Ground-based participants included the Lithuanian Air Force air defence battalion equipped with NASAMS, the Royal Netherlands Air Force equipped with MIM-104 PATRIOT and the Lithuanian Air Operations Centre. FAP F-16s and Spanish EF-18M Hornets integrated with the ground-based air defence units, complementing their capabilities and training readiness and reaction time to advanced air threats. During the closing ceremony on July 22, some airmen from the FAP BAP detachment were honoured for their performance in the exercise.

F-16AM 15101 inside a hardened aircraft prior to the long flight to Keflavik Air Base, Iceland for NATO air policing duty. Josef Campion

Portuguese Air Force F-16AM 15101 and an F-16BM break for the camera during a training mission flown from Base Aérea 5 Monte Real. Josef Campion

PORTUGAL'S FUTURE FIGHTER

In a December 2025 interview with Portuguese newspaper *Diário de Notícias*, General João Guilherme Cartaxo Alves, Chief of Staff of FAP, discussed the plans to renew its fighter fleet comprising 25 F-16AM and F-16BM jets: "The issue of replacing the F-16 should have been started 20 years ago. We received our F-16s when Denmark and Norway did and we are all at the same stage. Most of these countries started their replacement process in 2008-2009 and now it's 2025. FAP has never had an aircraft in active service for so many consecutive years: 31 years in the case of the most recent ones and almost 40 years in the case of the oldest from the second batch of F-16s."

Alves emphasised that FAP is only looking at new fighter aircraft that's one generation above the current one. Discussing the quantity and cost, he said: "The numbers will fluctuate between 14 and 28 fighters, roughly. These numbers tend to remain, regardless of the solution chosen. Regarding cost, whether it is the F-35 or any other capability, the values are very similar, between €3-4.8 billion. There has been reference to values in the order of €5 billion, but the essential thing is to realise that, within this range, the numbers do not differ that much between solutions."

Fighting 40th

Insight into the developmental operations conducted by the 40th Flight Test Squadron at Eglin Air Force Base, Florida.

An F-16C assigned to the 40th Flight Test Squadron during a test of an AGR-20 APKWS rocket on the Eglin range. USAF/TSgt John Raven

Major Johannes Weinberg serves as the F-16 division chief with the 40th Flight Test Squadron (FLTS) tasked with long-range test planning, interacting with customers and executing tests. That means making sure the aircrew selected are current and able to execute the tests, smartly scheduling the tests within the squadron's programme, conducting the debrief and ensuring any lessons learned are incorporated in future tests.

There are three Eglin-based stakeholders involved with each test: the 780th Test Squadron (see panel) which conducts air-to-air and air-to-ground munitions testing, the Air Force Seek Eagle Office (see panel) which is custodian of the safety aspects of loading stores and weapons on to an aircraftand the OFP Combined Test Force (see panel).

Explaining the role of each stakeholder, Weinberg said: "Usually, both request specific work directly with the 40th FLTS, but requests can also arrive from organisations from another off-base location such as the F-16 System Program Office based at Wright-Patterson Air Force Base, Ohio. Either organisation provides an outline of what they required the 40th FLTS to undertake and the primary data required for capture during the test events. Once defined, we enter the test planning phase. We use a standard process, which starts by determining how we will test the system or weapon, which is reviewed by multiple people working for the 40th FLTS.

"A primary engineer and project aircrew are assigned for the duration of the project. Depending on the test's complexity, a flight-test build-up is used, typically starting with the least complex working to the most complex. We use a software integration lab to ensure item works in the lab before it's fitted on an aircraft. Once installed, the item is tested while the aircraft is on the ground before flight testing begins. Issues are flushed out as the complexity of the different types of testing conducted by the 40th in accordance with the customer's requirements, within the performance bounds of the F-16."

The 40th's primary work is that of flight sciences, mostly at the request of the Air Force Seek Eagle Office, to determine that when loaded on the aircraft a new store will fit, be compatible and safe. Safety is determined by flying a series of missions in a flutter campaign.

Flutter is a dangerous, aeroelastic instability where external stores (missiles, bombs, fuel tanks) or structural components (wings and tail) on military aircraft vibrate uncontrollably, potentially leading to catastrophic structural failure. It occurs when aerodynamic forces, structural elasticity and inertial forces couple at high speeds, causing oscillations to grow rapidly rather than damp out.

Flutter and a phenomenon called limit cycle oscillation cause the wings to rapidly fluctuate in amplitude depending on the given flight conditions. Over time, the two phenomena can lead to fatigue of the wings and cracking,

The pilot of an F-16C assigned to the 40th Flight Test Squadron releases a stand-in attack weapon for the first time on November 7, 2024. USAF/SSgt Blake Wiles

which will lead to additional maintenance actions later. Testers characterise the phenomena in flight test missions, so the aircraft's flight envelope can be determined in terms of allowable G, altitude, airspeed and Mach.

Assuming a constant amplitude, if limit cycle oscillation goes unchecked, a flutter can grow to the point where wings rip off an aircraft. To prevent such a catastrophic event happening, aircraft assigned to the 40th FLTS are instrumented so that everything that's recorded by the aircraft is also being sent to a control room. Aircraft assigned to the 40th FLTS also carry accelerometers fitted on the wings and other stations. All data is downlinked to a control room, so the flight test team has as much – and sometimes more – situational awareness of what's happening with the aircraft than the pilots may have while flying.

The 40th FLTS is currently conducting a flutter campaign for the latest variant of the AGM-88 advanced anti-radiation guided missile (AARGM) used for the roles dubbed suppression and destruction of enemy air defences (SEAD/DEAD). Explaining the ongoing process, Major Weinberg said: "Given the construct of an F-16's wings, we will determine the approved munitions configurations and their corresponding envelopes. In certain cases, flying with asymmetric stores or without wingtip missiles can exacerbate flutter."

AGM-88J STAND-IN ATTACK WEAPON

Northrop Grumman's AGM-88J SiAW is an air-to-ground strike missile designed to destroy rapidly relocatable targets, including theatre ballistic missile launchers, cruise missile launchers, anti-ship missile launchers, GPS-jamming platforms and anti-satellite systems in contested environments. It is a direct development of the AGM-88G advance anti-radiation guided missile – extended range (AARGM-ER), being a specialised missile designed for a broader range of targets to include heavily defended land targets. The missile was designed using digital engineering and features open architecture interfaces that will allow for rapid subsystem upgrades to field enhanced capabilities. AGM-88J is specifically designed to fit within the internal weapon bays of the F-35 Lightning II. The first test articles were delivered to the USAF in November 2024, with initial operational capability currently planned for 2026.

An AIM-9X Sidewinder is shot off the rail of an F-16 over White Sands test range in New Mexico, on April 24, 2019. This marked the first time a Sidewinder had been used against a QF-16 full-scale aerial target. USAF/TSgt John Raven

The Air Force Seek Eagle Office also tasks the 40th FLTS with aircraft store compatibility testing to ensure that external or internal stores (weapons, fuel tanks, pods) can be safely carried and released from the aircraft without compromising safety or performance. It involves wind tunnel testing, computational fluid dynamics, structural analysis and flight tests. This determines what the flight profile and environments are when loaded with a new store. Weinberg said: "We fly the new store loaded on an F-16 to the edges of the aircraft's

F-16S WITH VENOM

The 96th Test Wing and 53rd Wing received the first three of six F-16s to be modified for the Viper Experimentation and Next-Gen Operations Model – Autonomy Flying Testbed (VENOM-AFT) programme. In an April 2024 press release, Major Ross Elder, VENOM developmental test lead with the 40th FLTS, described the programme as transformative: "The programme holds the potential to redefine air combat paradigms by fostering novel autonomous functions for current and future crewed and uncrewed platforms."

VENOM will undergo developmental and operational testing with the 40th Flight Test Squadron and the 85th Test and Evaluation Squadron, respectively. Operators from both squadrons will provide feedback to developers during modelling, simulation and post-flight to improve performance over time and ensure the autonomic system is making the appropriate decisions prior to and during a mission. The VENOM programme's goal is to enable the USAF to rapidly iterate and expand the body of knowledge for potential autonomy and payload solutions.

The last of the six F-16s selected for VENOM modification landed at Eglin on April 1, 2025. Modifications include installation of an auto-throttle to enable the autonomic system to regulate the flight control surfaces and the thrust. Explaining the objective, Major Trent McMullen, the 40th Flight Test Squadron's advanced capabilities division chief, said: "Modifying the aircraft is the result of a rigorous design phase and brings us one step closer to testing autonomy on a fighter jet with real mission systems and capabilities."

The autonomy system undergoes testing in faster-than-real-time modelling and simulation environments during countless combat scenarios. Simulations began in 2024 and included one-on-one and subsequently two-on-two scenarios involving within-visual-range and beyond-visual-range engagements. Captured data was analysed to help test engineers improve the autonomy.

Detailing the simulations, Major McMullen said: "Simulations provide an efficient way to train the autonomy to learn complex air combat tactics. A specific scenario can be run 1,000 times and the variations and decisions made throughout that mission can be studied. We then make recommendations to the developers on how to improve the autonomy's behaviour and overall performance."

The next step for VENOM development was software-in-the-loop testing, in which test engineers sought to ensure the VENOM autonomy connected to and communicated with the aircraft's system. Hardware testing was primarily focused on safety, for which test engineers confirmed that autonomous commands would not damage the aircraft or harm the pilot. Software and hardware testing both ensured the autonomy did not exceed its limits or its flight envelope regardless of the commands received.

The tests were completed in an F-16 flight simulator and were deemed critical for the human-in-the-loop role required for the VENOM programme. During flight testing, the ability to start and stop the autonomy in real time was critical. Hardware tests examined how to manage aggressive aircraft manoeuvres within the pilot's physical and physiological safety limits. Once software and hardware testing were cleared, the VENOM programme started ground testing using a fully modified F-16.

The VENOM programme was undergoing simultaneous developmental (DT) and operational (OT) testing at Eglin, with pilots working, flying and collaborating on missions, a methodology designed to reduce stove-piping of knowledge and lessons learned. McMullen said: "As the VENOM programme's first flight approaches, we are excited to test novel autonomous solutions. The strides we've witnessed in the simulated environment suggest VENOM will help advance aerial combat capabilities for future crewed and uncrewed platforms."

The Eglin-based 96th Test Wing and 53rd Wing welcomes the first three F-16s, which will be used in the Viper Experimentation and Next-Generation Operations Model autonomy flying testbed programme dubbed VENOM. USAF/David Shelikoff

ALQ-257 IVEWS

With a combined fleet of F-16 aircraft shared with the 85th Test and Evaluation Squadron, some are equipped with the ALQ-257 integrated Viper electronic warfare system (IVEWS) self-protection system which provides digital radar warnings and active jamming capability to detect, identify, locate and counter potential threats. The Eglin-based OFP squadrons are currently working to propagate the IVEWS system to the combat air forces (CAF).

Visually, an IVEWS-equipped F-16 can be identified by the intake lights that extend outward and around the fuselage. Discussing his squadron's ongoing work with IVEWS, Weinberg said: "IVEWS is still undergoing flight tests, with concurrent work underway to determine how to field the system. A lead engineer assigned to the OFP CTF is usually on hand for test events – sometimes customer representatives as well – and contractor personnel from Northrop Grumman. Being able to ask questions to these people is beneficial, especially during the brief. For example, what should the pilot expect to do at a specific point in time when working through the test cards during the flight? They usually know the answer and, if not, can ask somebody who does – likely somebody who coded the software.

"There's usually a lot of modifications fitted on the aircraft such as new instrumentation or new systems. These require maintenance actions. So, at any given time, if one of the F-16s fitted with IVEWS is down for maintenance actions, we may not be able to execute any testing that requires the system on at least one aircraft in the flight. Qualitatively, IVEWS is nice to have, because some of the legacy jammers used by the F-16 were developed back in the 1970s and 1980s."

In September 2024, an F-16 assigned to the 85th Test and Evaluation Squadron flew the first IVEWS OT flight at Eglin.

OFP combined test force

Another organisation that tasks the 40th FLTS with test work is the OFP combined test force (CTF), which is a unique dual-major command unit, collaborating with Air Combat Command's 53rd Wing, the 85th Test and Evaluation Squadron and Air Force Material Command's 96th Test Wing and the 40th Flight Test Squadron, both based at Eglin.

A second OT squadron assigned to the 53rd Wing is the 422nd TES based at Nellis Air Force Base, Nevada, which also collaborates with the OFP CTF. For completeness, the 40th FLTS has a sister DT squadron, the 416th FLTS based at Edwards Air Force Base, California, which supports some USAF F-16 testing but does not directly collaborate with the OFP CTF because it focuses on F-16 flight testing for foreign military sales (FMS) customers. Despite the extensive range supported by Edwards, Eglin operates the US Department of War's largest networked air-to-ground range and the Eglin Gulf Testing and Training Range for air-to-air weapon testing.

The CTF comprises aircrew, engineers, programme managers, analysts, maintenance and security personnel, who develop test concepts, prepare test plans and conduct end-to-end DT and OT for software and hardware upgrades on F-15 and F-16 aircraft. At Eglin, both the 40th FLTS and the 85th TES operate from the same building and their respective personnel work side-by-side to provide the capability to plan and execute testing, mitigate risk and deal with uncertainty, primarily with immature systems. Compared with the 40th's role, the 85th's task is to determine how and when a system or weapon can be utilised.

Weinberg said: "Tasking received from the OFP CTF usually begins with the 40th FLTS flying a safety of flight mission to check that the test store is safe to fly. A series of check flights are undertaken by an integrated test team with DT and OT pilots flying together, especially for some of the OFP and IVEWS tests before it is released to ops. When two F-16s are involved, we try to have one DT and one OT pilot flying the test because each offers a unique perspective on the system, then it's over to OT. For example, we've flown a test using a two-seat F-16D with a CDU installed in the aft cockpit as an upgrade. When new pilots are going through the F-16 B-course with a CDU fitted in the aft cockpit, they will gain experience of the new advanced capes for the first time during the course and not when they fly a single-seat F-16C for the first time.

"The safety of flight missions with the aft cockpit CDU was conducted to ensure that all the basic F-16 functions that a pilot needs to fly safely worked correctly and that the functionality provided by the new software-hardware package was as intended. Completing all test points enabled us to deem the aft cockpit CDU as being safe to fly, which means DT and OT pilots can fly that aircraft.

"For some of the specific flight sciences testing, our objective is to determine if there's a safe envelope for the store under test. We can't release the store to our colleagues in OT until such time that DT has completed the envelope expansion testing. We use a software integration lab (SIL) to complete much of the ground testing. In the case of the current flutter campaign for the AGM-88 SiAW, AFSEO conducted modelling and simulation based on the measured mass properties received from a precision measurement facility. But determining how the store will integrate with the aircraft's OFP, and how the store should be loaded into the stores management system, is determined in collaboration with the OT folks. And in the case of IVEWS, collaboration also includes the Northrop Grumman personnel who are developing the software and hardware and concurrently testing it in the SIL.

"Nearly all of our flights are test missions, during which we capture data. Over a long-timespan, over multiple flights and during multiple hours, we document any issues to determine the item's suitability. We ask questions. Are there going to be problems in the future? Is the item going to lead to more faults and failures that will require more maintenance actions before we release it to OT?"

Concluding, Major Weinberg said that serving with the 40th FLTS affords a connection with operations and the CAF: "Whenever we have questions – such as what is happening in operations right now or what are the relevant needs? – our OT colleagues can provide us with the information. Or we can ask them about current tactics, which they can explain and demonstrate to us. Such actions keep us DT folks better connected to the airmen serving in the CAF and keeps them in the forefront of our minds for all the tests we execute. Bear in mind that we conduct testing to enhance the capability and the lethalness of airmen and the military at large."

envelope to ensure the store continues to function. Using high resolution photos, the test team documents what the store looks like before and after the flight to determine if the store moves on its pylon in flight, that no panels fall off and that all software and hardware still work after the store has been stressed."

Most commonly, the 40th FLTS tests a new software package for an existing type of pod, primarily to make sure the pod still functions. For example, will an existing pod system loaded with a new release of software still generate co-ordinates at the required quality. Pods carried by the F-16 include the AAQ-33 Sniper targeting pod used for high-fidelity, long-range identification and precision target designation; the ALQ-131 and ALQ-184 electronic

A test pilot from the 40th Flight Test Squadron fires an AGR-20 APKWS rocket from his F-16 against a stationary target on the Eglin range on November 3, 2020. USAF/TSgt John Raven

The crew of an F-16D prepare to drop two collaborative small diameter bombs (marked with yellow stripes) at White Sands in New Mexico on December 13, 2020. USAF/TSgt John McRell

An F-16 assigned to the 85th Test and Evaluation Squadron powers down after flying with the ALQ-257 integrated Viper electronic warfare suite for the first time. USAF/1st Lt Rebecca Abordo

AIR FORCE SEEK EAGLE OFFICE

The Air Force Seek Eagle Office (AFSEO) is part of the 96th Test Wing based at Eglin Air Force Base, Florida, and serves as the centre of expertise for the Seek Eagle programme. The AFSEO leverages data to conduct aircraft-store compatibility (ASC) engineering and maintains the Seek Eagle data repository, to ensure safe and acceptable aircraft-store combinations in accordance with military standards, handbooks and best practices.

The Seek Eagle programme manages a standardised framework for ensuring the safe and effective integration of stores (weapons, pods, etc) with aircraft. It follows a step-by-step methodology as defined by regulations and guidelines which outline the procedures, evaluations and analyses required to certify that an aircraft can safely and effectively carry, release, load and unload a particular store.

AFSEO is designated by the Secretary of the Air Force as the primary source for certification technical support and the central repository for all data gathered from store testing. Aircraft and store programme offices are required to provide all USAF aircraft-store compatibility engineering data to the AFSEO, regardless of whether the AFSEO's services are directly utilised. AFSEO's assigned team of engineers, analysts and support staff conducts evaluations, maintains the data repository, provides technical expertise and issues recommendations to aircraft system programme offices to support DT, OT and fielding of aircraft-store systems.

The AFSEO utilises a wide range of engineering disciplines and tools to generate engineering rationale and recommendations, including wind tunnel testing, fitting and functional checks, modelling and simulation and data analysis. The engineering core comprises technical teams with expertise in the following areas: store fit, ballistics, store carriage and release, combat weapons delivery software, soft release and information-based tools.

***Store fit** includes a comprehensive database of 3D aircraft and store models, computerised fit checks and assessment of store fit through models created from engineering drawings or photogrammetry.*

***Ballistics** includes a database of aerodynamic and ballistic information for munitions, mathematical modelling for fuse arming and function and software verification/validation for the weapon delivery portion of operational flight programmes.*

***Store carriage and release** covers aircraft and store loads, aircraft flutter, vibration, aircraft stability and control, store separation analysis, ground and flight test support and electromagnetic interference/compatibility.*

***Combat weapons delivery software** functions as a single source for aircraft delivery planning, covering all fighter and bomber mission planning in the USAF, supporting a wide range of munitions, and incorporates USAF-certified safe escape and separation methodology. Safe escape defines minimum release altitudes, safe separation times for safe fuse arming and test, chase plane and aircraft deconfliction analysis.*

***Information-based tools** include historical data on thousands of compatibility actions for use to clear new configurations by analogy, and store mass and physical measurement in a computerised library containing more than 1,500 types of stores.*

An F-16C of the 40th FLTS with a stand-in attack weapon loaded on station 3 during the first test shot mission on November 7, 2024. USAF/SSgt Blake Wiles

countermeasure pods designed to jam enemy radars and the ASQ-213 HARM Targeting System used to target AGM-88 HARM missiles. The 40th also tests new types of pods."

In addition to performing flight sciences testing, the 40th FLTS also conducts weapons testing, a tasking usually received from the 780th Test Squadron (see panel). A recent weapon test project involved AGM-88J stand-in attack weapon (SiAW) released from an F-16, one to demonstrate the store could be jettisoned and a series to ensure the test vehicle correctly releases from the aircraft in its envelope. Discussing the separation test, Weinberg said: "The instrumented test vehicle separated from the pylon within all the known parameters, which gave the test team a sufficient amount of confidence that a test vehicle would not hit the aircraft after separation. A separation test campaign continues using fully configured missiles with a sensor suite installed."

The first release of an AGM-88J jettison test vehicle (JTV), one with no rocket motor or internal electronics installed, was successfully released over the Gulf of Mexico from a 40th Flight Test Squadron F-16 on November 7, 2024. A JTV is used specifically to determine whether the weapon safely separates from the aircraft upon a commanded release. The November 7 test was successful and a major milestone that enabled further testing to begin.

According to a release issued by Northrop Grumman at the time, Colonel Gary Roos, senior materiel leader for the Adaptive Weapons Division at the Air Force Life Cycle Management Center, said: "The separation test of SiAW from an F-16 is intended to provide

96TH TEST WING

The 96th Test Wing at Eglin Air Force Base, Florida, is the test and evaluation centre for USAF air-delivered weapons, navigation and guidance systems, command and control systems and Air Force Special Operations Command systems. The wing provides expert evaluation and validation of the performance of systems throughout the design, development, acquisition and sustainment process to ensure airmen have technologically superior, reliable, maintainable, sustainable and safe systems.

The unit performs developmental test and evaluation across the complete system lifecycle for a wide variety of customers, including the System Program Offices, the Air Force Research Laboratory, logistics and product centres, major commands, other Department of War services foreign military sales and private industry. It conducts developmental test and evaluation to enable airmen to put weapons on target in all battlespace media and as the installation host wing, provide support for all other missions conducted at Eglin.

The 96th Operations Group conducts the wing's primary missions of developmental testing and evaluation of conventional munitions, command and control systems, A-10 and F-15 avionics and navigation and guidance systems. It manages 20 instrumented F-15C, F-15E, F-15EX, F-16C and UH-1N test aircraft maintained by the 96th Maintenance Group.

Other groups assigned to the wing are the 96th Mission Support Group, 96th Medical Group, 96th Civil Engineer Group and 96th Range Group. The last of these operates, maintains and protects the Eglin Gulf Test Range, comprising approximately 120,000 square miles of overwater airspace, covering the eastern third of the Gulf of Mexico from the Florida panhandle to the Florida Keys. The land range covers 724 square miles and contains 70 specific test and training areas, including the only qualified air-to-ground supersonic range east of the Mississippi river.

The wing's test and evaluation capabilities focus on non-nuclear munitions, including ballistics, guidance and terminal effects, munitions ground testing including modelling, simulation and analysis, munitions seeker performance evaluation including electro-optical, infrared, millimetre wave, radio frequency and laser sensors, aircraft stores integration, command, control and information testing, computer network attack, aircraft systems and electronic countermeasure evaluation, munitions and aircraft navigation and guidance systems, radar target signatures including very low observables and antenna pattern measurements, unmanned aerial vehicle; and base intrusion and interdiction systems.

An F-16C aircraft assigned to the 40th Flight Test Squadron taxies at Andersen Air Force Base, Guam, on July 12, 2025, during the first USAF Department-Level Exercise series dubbed Resolute Force Pacific 2025. USAF/Senior Airman Jade Caldwell

780TH TEST SQUADRON

As the munitions test experts for the 96th Test Wing, the 780th Test Squadron is responsible for most of the developmental testing of USAF conventional weapons. Its role is to manage, plan and execute test programmes for customers that are largely from the Systems Program Offices and the Air Force Research Laboratory at Eglin. Both the 40th FLTS and 413th FLTS provide the test pilots, aircrew and aircraft for weapons testing, while the 780th provides the programme and test engineers to lead, plan and execute the weapon tests.

The 780th TS is divided into three main weapons test divisions: air-to-air, air-to-surface and ground. A weapons effects flight interacts with all three divisions, primarily providing oversight for live-fire test and evaluation. Ground weapons tests includes sled track testing, arena testing, static explosions, guns and ammunition. A sled test simulates air impact parameters by delivering a warhead down the Eglin sled track into a realistic target at operational velocities and impact angles to collect warhead/fuse survivability and functionality information. It's all part of risk reduction. An arena test involves a test item placed within a unique target with instrumentation, followed by a remote detonation to collect vulnerability and lethality information. Flight testing involves carrying the weapon on an aircraft. The AFSEO conducts analysis to predict whether the bomb and rack will fly and release safely. In some cases, the 780th executes compatibility flight profiles with the weapon loaded on the aircraft to make sure it is safe to carry.

The 780th TS consists primarily of programme and test engineers who are assigned to run the mission. A programme engineer deals mainly with documentation, funding and scheduling with the customer. Test engineers work with the aircrews and range personnel, write the flight cards and perform the planning and execution of the test. Once planning is complete and documents are signed, there are several milestones to achieve: safety board and flight clearance and ultimately giving the brief to the 96th Operations Group commander, who must approve any flight test.

During a flight test, the 780th has an engineer in the control room on the ground who orchestrates the entire mission, while flight test engineers fly in the back seat of the aircraft to assist the test pilo, providing in-flight expertise gained from their detailed involvement with the technical and programme planning. A flight test engineer provides a critical link between the discipline engineers and operations personnel, helping them understand detailed engineering specifications in line with what's possible in a practical operations environment.

An F-16C aircraft assigned to the 20th Fighter Wing on the hot cargo pad loaded with AGR-20F APKWS rockets at Shaw Air Force Base, South Carolina, on June 11, 2025. USAF/Airman 1st Class Nyanda Walker-Potts

AGR-20F FALCO

In 2016, the 96th Test Wing devised a rapid fielding plan for the AGR-20 Advanced Precision Kill Weapon System II that turns existing Hydra 70 unguided rockets into precision-guided munitions through the addition of a laser guidance kit. APKWS offers a multi-shot capability and limits collateral damage in close combat.

That July, a flight test team comprising personnel from the 40th FLTS and the Air National Guard Air Force Reserve Test Center based at Morris ANG Base in Tucson, Arizona, flew seven missions with A-10 and F-16 aircraft. Missions included minimum and maximum range, ripple release and trajectory shaping tests against a variety of realistic targets selected to validate the rocket's capability. The team achieved 14 successful shots.

Initially, the AGR-20 APKWS provided the A-10 and F-16 with bigger weapons loads, enabling pilots to engage more targets, especially in the CAS role. The latest version, designated the AGR-20F Fixed-wing, Air-Launched, Counter-Unmanned Aircraft System (FALCO), was developed as a rapid solution to counter cheap loitering munitions, drone swarms and cruise missiles, particularly those used by the Houthi rebels in Yemen and the Red Sea and by Iranian-backed groups.

An AGR-20F uses a long-wave infrared (LWIR) seeker and a dual-safe proximity fuse for better accuracy against manoeuvring targets without the need for a constant laser designation. Launched from F-16s and F-15Es, an AGR-20F rocket can fly at speeds near Mach 2.9, with a range of several miles, to destroy drones in the counter-unmanned aerial systems (C-UAS) role. Flight testing for the C-UAS role began in 2019, the year the USAF first demonstrated the rocket's air-to-air capability, when an F-16C fired a rocket against a BQM-167 target drone to simulate intercepting low-flying cruise missiles.

On December 19, 2019, the 85th Test and Evaluation Squadron shot down a drone using an AGR-20A APKWS laser-guided rocket cued by an F-16 targeting pod as a proof of concept for using rockets as viable munitions to perform cruise missile defence (CMD). An APKWS rocket is more cost-effective for the CMD role than an AIM-120 AMRAAM, which was a key requirement. Additionally, AGR-20A rockets can be loaded faster than AIM-120s and multiple rockets can be loaded rapidly into tube launchers, providing a loadout two-to-three times the number of missiles.

In March 2023, the testing division of the US Army Joint C-UAS Office based at Fort Sill, Oklahoma, successfully tested the AGR-20F APKWS against drones traveling at more than 100mph.

The AGR-20F is designed to engage Group 2 and Group 3 drones, providing a low-cost alternative to expensive, traditional air-to-air missiles. A Group 2 drone is medium-sized, weighs 21-55lb, and operates below 3,500ft at speeds under 250kt, such as the ScanEagle. A Group 3 drone is larger, weighs less than 1,320lb, operates below 18,000ft at speeds under 250kt, such as an RQ-7 Shadow.

During 2023-2024, USAF F-15E and F-16 aircraft employed AGR-20 APKWS rockets to shoot down Houthi-launched drones.

the validation of the weapon's safe separation characteristics and generate invaluable data for optimising its performance. The results can reinforce SiAW's ability to provide a critical advantage to airmen in the face of evolving threats."

Northrop Grumman's vice president of advanced weapons, Chuck Johnson, said: "With the insights [gained] from the separation test, we will continue the missile's development and ultimately, deliver a critical capability to airmen. Our work ensures the USAF will have a highly survivable precision strike weapon that will meet current and future mission needs."

Explaining other aspects of the 40th's test role, Major Weinberg said one separate division tests advanced capabilities using F-16s. Currently, its primary focus is the VENOM programme and risk reduction work for co-operative combat aircraft: "Because the F-16 is a cost-effective aircraft to fly, the USAF uses the type to fly chase with other aircraft types, most commonly during weapon integration testing. So, for example, we can fly chase to make sure the launch aircraft can safely release the weapon and then safely recover. We also perform photo chase for store separation using high-speed cameras mounted on and forward and aft of stations one and nine. Whenever the F-16 pilot selects the pickle button, the cameras start recording. Imagery recorded is used by the test team to characterise the store's separation from the aircraft. If a budget is not available for using an aircraft mounted with the cameras, we can fly missions using a two-seat F-16D with a photographer in the back seat. Our photographers use handheld high-speed cameras to film the separation of the munition or firing in the case of a missile

An F-16C assigned to the 20th Fighter Wing fitted with a rocket launcher pod loaded with six AGR-20F APKWS rockets. USAF/Airman 1st Class Nyanda Walker-Potts

An F-16D assigned to the 40th Flight Test Squadron over the Gulf of Mexico. USAF/SSgt Blake Wiles

RAYTHEON PHANTOMSTRIKE RADAR

According to Raytheon, its PhantomStrike radar unit weighs half the weight of a modern AESA radar, at less than 150lb. Capabilities include digital beam forming and steering, multimode functionality and interleaved ground and air targeting. The radar uses a first-of-its-kind air-cooled design dubbed CHIRP, which combines Gallium nitride-power and innovative packaging of its digital receiver/exciter and processor providing what Raytheon cites as unparalleled performance in a compact form.

Aircrew of an F-16D assigned to the 40th Flight Test Squadron look at the photo-ship aircraft while flying over the Gulf of Mexico on September 16, 2025. USAF/SSgt Thomas Barley

and capture data about the separation from the chase aircraft."

One change that improves execution of flight testing undertaken by all USAF DT and OT F-16 squadrons is the Operational Flight Program (OFP) software coding. This is no longer undertaken by Lockheed Martin but by USAF personnel. Describing the change, Weinberg said: "This is a huge improvement because our in-house personnel can refine and quickly iterate software to deliver new capabilities to airmen much more quickly. For the F-16, we're currently running M8.2.6, a test release of the OFP, which will be followed in the next 12 months by M8.2.7. The rate of new releases depends on the progress of the Software Engineering Group based at Hill Air Force Base to incorporate new features and fixes to the OFP."

The 40th FLTS also conducts test campaigns to fulfil urgent operational needs (UONs), specific capabilities required by operational units, and by the very nature of a UON, delivering the testing expeditiously with more acceptance of risk. One example is the FALCO programme, which sought to utilise an AGR-20 APKWS rocket to shoot down a drone. Another UON currently in testing with the 40th FLTS is for the rapid development of the AGM-188A extended range attack missile. Its capability criteria are for striking high-value fixed targets from stand-off range with precision guidance at an affordable cost. A flutter campaign is currently underway, which Major Weinberg described as a behemoth: "It takes a lot of flights and a lot of resources to be able to clear out that store."

AGM-188A ERAM

On January 21, 2026, the 40th FLTS launched an extended range attack munition (ERAM), a stand-off cruise missile with a live-warhead, on the Eglin Test and Training Range. The event took place less than 16 months from the programme's initial contract award.

ERAM is a cost-effective, next-generation, precision-guided, stand-off air-launched cruise missile designed to destroy high-value fixed targets and can be rapidly produced in large numbers to meet an urgent operational requirement. Designated the AGM-188A, the munition is a 500lb missile, powered by a TJ80 turbojet, with a significant range. The programme was initiated to deliver a low-cost, air-launched and lightweight cruise missile to Ukraine.

On August 28, 2025, the US Defense Security Cooperation Agency posted a release that the US State Department had approved a possible foreign military sale to Ukraine of air-delivered munitions and related equipment for an estimated cost of $825m. It stated: "Funding from Denmark, the Netherlands, Norway and foreign military financing from the US is being used by Ukraine for the purchase. Ukraine requested to buy up to 3,350 ERAM missiles and 3,350 embedded GPS/INS units with selective availability anti-spoofing modules. The missiles will improve Ukraine's capability to meet threats by further equipping it to conduct self-defence and regional security missions. The principal contractors will be Zone 5 Technologies and CoAspire."

According to Eglin Air Force Base: "The test was a collaborative effort between the Air Force Life Cycle Management Center's Armament Directorate, the 96th Test Wing and industry partners. Engineers and test conductors from Eglin's Central Control Facility planned the mission and analysed the data, leveraging the Eglin Test and Training Range's capabilities to facilitate the complex event."

Outlining the live test, Brigadier General Mark Massaro, commander of the 96th Test Wing, said: "The future fight demands we create an asymmetric advantage by developing cost-effective, attritable systems like ERAM that give commanders the ability to generate mass. This test was a critical milestone on that path. The expert teams who executed this complex mission provided the high-fidelity data we need to validate this system [the live missile met all its primary objectives including a full warhead detonation], ensuring that when it reaches the warfighter, it is a proven and ready tool for the right target. This is the cornerstone of building a more lethal and effective joint force."

Black Sheep

A report on the F-16-equipped 8th Fighter Squadron, the only remaining squadron based at Holloman Air Force Base, New Mexico, that once flew the F-117 Nighthawk stealth fighter.

The 8th Fighter Squadron is one of three assigned to the 54th Fighter Group at Holloman Air Force Base dedicated to training F-16 pilots, instructor pilots and those requalifying. The 54th FG trains an average of 180 students per year, averaging more than 10,800 sorties and 14,600 hours. Half of the USAF's new F-16 pilots are trained by the 54th every year, which equates to about 25% of all its fighter pilots.

The 8th FS has 50 personnel and 24 Block 42 F-16s assigned. During an average week the squadron flies 100 sorties, depending on the weather and other external factors. Located in the desert of western New Mexico, the White Sands Missile Range is the primary airspace used by all the 54th Fighter Group's fighter squadrons.

White Sands allows the squadrons to train student pilots against an accurate representation of the next generation of threats, helping them prepare for their next unit. It enables pilots to operate up to 50,000ft with areas that permit supersonic flight. It's located immediately to the northwest of the base, so all training flights enter the airspace minutes after take-off from Holloman.

FLIGHT OPERATIONS

There are five squadrons assigned to the 54th Fighter Group: the 8th, 311th and the 314th Fighter Squadrons, the 54th Training Squadron (TS) and the 54th Operations Support Squadron (OSS). The 54th OSS is responsible for the airfield, the control tower and training, and – unique for an OSS – liaison with the White Sands Missile Range. This includes airspace scheduling, co-ordination and deconfliction, which is a huge task.

Students begin their training with the 54th TS, completing academics, emergency procedures training and simulator training over 6-8 weeks. The 54th TS also runs the human weapon system programme (HWSP) in which certified instructors and physical therapists devise workout programmes to improve pilot health and injury prevention. HWSP provides a student with their first introduction on how to take care of their bodies in a very stressful flight environment and regime. Students then move

F-16C 88-517/HO parked on the 8th Fighter Squadron flight line at Holloman. Tail markings include a stylised yellow tail stripe featuring an outline of an F-117 Nighthawk. Mark Ayton

on to one of the three fighter squadrons, where they undertake all their follow-on training until the end of the B Course over seven-and-a-half months, not least their first flight in an F-16.

B COURSE

As squadron commander, Lieutenant Colonel Matthew Marshall and his staff run the Air Education and Training Command's F-16 basic course, dubbed the B Course.

This comprises five phases:

- Transition
- Basic fighter manoeuvring (BFM)
- Tactical intercepts
- Basic surface attack
- Precision-guided weapon employment

The course culminates in a large force exercise in which the students fight their way to their assigned target, drop precision-guided bombs from medium altitude, then fight their way out.

TRANSITION AND BFM

Students start their course with six weeks of academic study before flying training begins – it's a scripted phase just like any other pipeline training. Simulators are interspersed throughout the course to introduce each new event and role.

The initial academics can often seem overwhelming to the student because there's a lot of workbooks, classes and simulators before the student can set foot in the jet. Students rely on civilian and military instructors who are well versed in how to make it make sense from the early stage.

In the first part, the student is introduced to the techniques required to take off, land, fly and cruise. Instructor pilots (IPs) follow the student around the airfield pattern and tell them to go around if they see something unsafe. Once a student pilot completes their check ride, they receive their initial Form 8, a certificate that shows they can safely pilot the aircraft in daytime visual and instrument conditions.

Students are then introduced to tactics, starting with basic fighter manoeuvring: low aspect, followed by high aspect and then nose-to-nose BFM. These require a wider array of personal techniques, imparted to the students by different IPs.

Generally, pilots say the F-16 is not too hard to learn to fly, but it's hard to learn how to fight. This is especially so when they are trying to use all the controls on the throttle and stick. The USAF uses a basic left hand-right hand instruction technique. An IP takes the student through the mission brief and instructs them at the start of the aerial battle to select max afterburner with their left hand and with their right hand to roll out and fly to where the adversary starts their turn. When the student reaches that point, they must start their turn by pulling to 9G with their right hand and relax to freeze the adversary so they can start to decrease angles, which will allow them to attack from a stable gunshot position. That sequence happens in about five to seven seconds, so their left and right hands and their brain will not be moving as fast as they need. Because of the air combat manoeuvring instrumentation system used by the USAF, the IP and the student can use the mission data recorded during the flight in the debrief. This enables the IP to identify when the student carried out their instructions. The student may have selected max afterburner a little too late or pulled too hard when they needed to relax and apply back-stick pressure instead of pointing at the adversary.

During BFM, the tactical portion lasts for no more than 20 minutes, but the debrief lasts about two hours. The 20-minute tactical portion in the first few BFM rides is a script. The student will likely be soaked in sweat and breathing hard and will be barely hanging on by the end. The IP must get the student to take a deep breath and prepare to return to Holloman and land just like they learned to do in the transition phase.

Students fly three offensive BFM flights and generally struggle with the first two, but on the third, nearly all students do better. Generally, students can keep up using the left hand-right hand mantra quite a bit more during the defensive BFM rides and most have figured things out by the end of the BFM phase.

AIR COMBAT MANOEUVRING

There are not many hours in the entire B Course training programme, so it is designed to cater for an average student, such that if an individual gets to the end of the BFM phase the IPs can safely move them onto air combat manoeuvring (ACM). This primarily comprises 2 v 1 and 2 v 2 engagements, which means the

When F-16s are repainted following program depot maintenance Have Glass paint is used. Mark Ayton

RESCUE
0769
1

F-16s assigned to the 8th Fighter Squadron returning from a Large Force Exercise mission at Homestead Air Reserve Base, Florida. USAF/MSgt Lionel Castellano

F-16D 88-161/HO assigned to the 8th Fighter Squadron taxis through a jet wash. USAF/Senior Airman Michelle Ferrari

student has a third and a fourth aircraft from which to deconflict.

As with the start of the BFM phase, IPs find that the student's left and right hands and their brain are moving slower than required, so IPs must figure out where the lags are and speed up the student's execution. The IPs try to make things as simple as they can for the students, so they have the brain capacity to keep up with what's going on. By primarily calling 'left hand, right hand' on the radio, the IP can get things to a simple state.

An IP can adapt each flight based on the student's ongoing performance. Some students perform so well that the IP can fly more aggressively against them – as if flying against another instructor. For students who are struggling, the IP keeps it simple and gets them to the minimum standard required by the USAF.

TACTICAL INTERCEPTS

Following ACM, students move on to long-range tactical intercepts (TIs), which trains them to use the radar to identify, target and shoot missiles to kill the adversary. Up until this point, the student has visually manoeuvred their aircraft in relation to another.

Students start with basic 1 v 1 long-range intercepts and then step-up to 2 v 2 and finally 4 v 4. In the complicated 4 v 4 scenarios, IPs want the student to remain in formation and follow the flight lead around as they execute the tactics. If the student can do that, it's nearly good enough. If the student can do that and take a shot or two, it's good. If the student can do that and shoot multiple contacts at the same time, they are doing well.

The TI phase culminates with a defensive counter air (DCA) mission in which the student is responsible for protecting a target. During the operation, adversaries may fly at low-level to test the student to look down low as per the radar tactics instruction given to them.

Before the DCA mission, IPs spend a significant amount of time teaching

An F-16D assigned to the 54th Fighter Group on a mission flown from Homestead Air Reserve Base, Florida, during a Large Force Exercise. USAF/Senior Airman Michelle Ferrari

academics and having informal one-on-one conversations with the students to ensure they understand what's going to happen, their responsibilities, the importance of the sortie and the instructor's expectations.

In the air-to-air portion, which represents about half the training programme, the aircraft is configured in one of two ways. One configuration is referred to as a centreline bag jet fitted with just one fuel tank on the centreline station (station 6). This configuration is used mostly for air-to-air training. The aircraft's configuration changes for the final portion of air-to-air training when the sorties are longer and require two external fuel tanks carried on under-wing stations 4 and 8, a configuration referred to as a two-bag jet.

AIR-TO-GROUND

Students conduct low-level step-down training to learn how to fly at 500ft and safely manoeuvre near the ground ahead of transitioning to the air-to-ground phase. The two-bag configuration is used throughout the air-to-ground phase.

When loaded with both laser- and GPS-guided bombs, the student is presented with a lot of information, much of which isn't relevant, so the IPs try to cage their brain into understanding what they must do to make the bomb hit their assigned target. IPs have extensive discussions with the student about what is considered a valid versus an invalid weapon employment. It's vital for the student to remember if they are dropping a GPS-guided weapon on a set of co-ordinates, so if they accidentally bump a switch they can induce a slew into the system, leaving the jet thinking the target is not at the point given by the co-ordinates.

Students must follow in-depth laser checks known as TCAS. T reminds them to switch the tapes on, C reminds them to place their cursor to zero to remove any slew out of the system, A reminds them to check the jet's altitude mode. The checks ensure that the pilot has the right laser code, with different aircraft in a flight having different laser codes. If a pilot laser-designates for one jet and then his own without resetting the laser coding for his jet, then the bomb will never detect the laser energy.

If a bomb malfunctions and doesn't go where it's supposed to, the tapes will be checked to make sure the pilot applied the TCAS checks properly. If the pilot doesn't complete a proper check, they could miss or kill innocent people. IPs must ensure each student completes the course fully with the understanding that when they hit the pickle button, they are striking the right target.

A primary role for the F-16 is close air support (CAS), which is introduced towards the end of the air-to-ground portion. Typically, the CAS missions are aligned with the final capstone large force employment exercise. For this, the student flies a strike mission as part of an eight-ship. Pilots must fight adversaries on the way into the target area, find the proper target, conduct the TCAS check, drop the valid weapon, then fight adversaries on the way out. It's also the capstone exercise for a trainee multi-role fighter pilot.

Explaining why the syllabus changes, Lieutenant Colonel Marshall said: "We take feedback from the combat air forces and

DEDICATED CREW CHIEF

A dedicated crew chief's role is multi-faceted. They make sure that everyone who works on a specific aircraft is safe and conduct a safety inspection before any kind of maintenance is undertaken.

SSgt Aaron Rodriguez Vasquez, a dedicated drew chief with the 8th Aircraft Maintenance Unit, explained: "We also work with production to identify scheduled inspections and with the back shops to schedule their respective inspections. I'm a flight line supervisor of a group of crew chiefs and ensure they are doing the right thing and in the right order."

Discussing the main requirement for a crew chief, SSgt Rodriguez Vasquez said: "Resilience, because our schedule moves back and forth, and a crew chief must be able to accept a jet that's got another issue – possibly the same issue – and fix it again. Because the jets are old, that aspect becomes more and more regular, and the jets generally fly twice a day, five times a week.

"To pick the most common recurring problem depends on the season – we have problems with the hydraulic system when the temperature gets too hot or cold. During my six years of experience, I've done a lot of things for other shops and I've learned the basic things they do. That subsequently saves me time, because I don't have to call someone from a back shop to fix the issue because I know how to carry out the work required. Changing a brake is something that's a simple task, but it's tedious because there are certain things you must do and you've got to work on a lot of hydraulic-powered systems. Once a brake is bad we've got to change it during the turn between flights.

"Being a crew chief is hard work. The hardest part is the sacrifice made with your family's time, but it's a very rewarding job."

F-16D 90-793/HO assigned to the 54th Fighter Group flies over Key West, Florida. USAF/Senior Airman Michelle Ferrari

F-16s assigned to the 54th Fighter Group fly over Key West during a Large Force Exercise at Homestead Air Reserve Base, Florida, on March 13, 2025. USAF/Senior Airman Michelle Ferrari

An F-16 Viper assigned to the 8th Fighter Squadron flies over Holloman Air Force Base, New Mexico, June 6, 2024. The squadron's flagship honours the F-117 Nighthawk, which was flown by the 8th FS for more than 25 years. US Air Force

BLACK SHEEP FLAGSHIP

During the early summer of 2024, the 8th Fighter Squadron collaborated with the Ogden Air Logistics Center at Hill Air Force Base, Utah, to paint its flagship aircraft in a matte black colour scheme in honour of the F-117 Nighthawk. Block 42 F-16C 88-0517/HO (c/n 1C-119) was delivered to Luke Air Force Base, Arizona, in March 1990. The combination of light and dark grey tones and the distinctive squadron markings give the aircraft a unique appearance. The flagship aircraft is utilised for air shows and any available opportunities to showcase the 8th FS heritage.

Major Daniel Thompson, an instructor pilot with the 8th FS, explained: "We were striving for a design that allowed the jet to perform in training and look good from all angles. Various concepts and modifications were implemented on the jet, leading to the final design, which was the product of extensive rumination within the squadron."

For more than 25 years, the 8th FS flew the F-117 on missions in high-threat environments to strike high-value targets with great precision while evading enemy defences. The squadron also played a crucial role in integrating the Nighthawk into the USAF's operational capabilities. Lieutenant Colonel Matthew Marshall said: "The heritage aircraft project started three years ago when I was the squadron's director of operations. It took a lot of time to get all the paperwork correct and get all the pieces in place to finally make it happen. The jet swap helped, because we were able to create a new flagship after the old one left. So when we were considering cool ideas and trying to promote the heritage of the USAF and our squadron, Major Thompson came up with the idea to paint the jet matte black and apply grey lines and the features of the F-117. I thought it was outstanding. We all really like the fact that it highlights our history and our heritage."

Afterburner operation occurs when jet fuel is injected into the engine augmenter, resulting in an exhaust flame. USAF/Airman 1st Class Michelle Ferrari

work through rewrites of the syllabus every couple of years. Tactics change based on the perceived threats we must train to for a great power competition against near peer adversaries. We must be prepared for the changing nature of the conflicts that the US and its allies might end up in, so we change what we're training people for. Overall, the initial qualification course [the B Course] tends to stay roughly the same. We teach a new pilot how to fly the jet, how to conduct dogfighting, how to do 2 v 1, how to do tactical intercepts – elements that stay the same. It's the numbers that change as the potential threats change."

The most significant addition in recent years has been precision-guided weapon delivery, the provision of more rounds for practising strafing and the close air support component.

MENTORING

Most pilots who qualify as instructors have the capability to mentor students. The difficulties of the job arise when a student has a few bad flights in a row. In the syllabus, the student could do well on Monday, but then be close to elimination from the programme by Thursday because of the permissible number of bust rides in place for non-progression.

An IP can be responsible for five pilots. Some of them may do well the whole time, others are up and down. IPs have closed-door discussions, which are off the record. An IP will relate to the trainee by letting them know that they were once in the same shoes as the student and had a hard time. An IP will also get the student to realise that they are expected to make mistakes, that it is OK and they must compartmentalise their errors. There is nothing the student can do because the mistake has happened and the individual must move on, either to the rest of the flight if they have made a mistake during a flight or to the next flight. An IP must always try to instil the ability to accept their mistakes, move on and get back to a positive attitude.

MISSION QUALIFICATION TRAINING

Before the course halfway point, the 8th FS co-ordinates with the 54th Fighter Group's personnel centre to determine the operational assignments for student pilots.

The basic course is followed by a further six weeks' training covering Block-specific avionics and mission systems. This is important for each pilot transferring to a combat air force unit operating a specific Block of aircraft, all of which have different configurations. Once a new pilot arrives at their operational unit, they spend up to 90 days completing initial mission qualification training (MQT). Completion of MQT qualifies them to deploy with their squadron and conduct combat tasking as a wingman.

PILOT OUTPUT

Lieutenant Colonel Marshall and his staff are tasked to produce new F-16 pilots, an objective accomplished by 40 personnel, excluding students, the 8th Aircraft Maintenance Unit and a fleet of 24 F-16s.

In 2023, Marshall and his staff were tasked to swap the squadron's fleet of Block 40 aircraft with Block 42s from Luke Air Force Base, Arizona. A Block 40 aircraft features the Pratt & Whitney F100-PW-220 engine, while a Block 42 is equipped with the General Electric F110-GE-129. The Luke-based 309th Fighter Squadron received Block 40 aircraft from the 8th Fighter Squadron in exchange for its Block 42 aircraft. The swap, which commenced on July 10, 2023, required a lot of work to inspect and accept the jets at both Holloman and Luke.

Providing some insight into the aircraft swap, Lieutenant Colonel Marshall said: "We had a B Course class that was getting ready to graduate with Block 40 aircraft. Our command

USAF/Senior Airman Chase Cannon

PRODUCTION SUPERINTENDENT

Master Sergeant Franco Molinaro is a production superintendent with the 311th Aircraft Maintenance Unit. He is responsible for flight line operations, overviews the maintenance state of all the jets and allocates them to the daily flight schedule and has input to scheduling the week's flying and long-term planning.

Discussing the production supervisor's role, Molinaro said: "The ability to prioritise, with the ability to understand what can be done now and what needs to be held off, is a primary requirement of my job. As a crew chief, if something doesn't get done, it is down to the crew chief. As a production supervisor, if something happens on the flight line, it's on me. As a production supervisor, I'm still heavily involved in aircraft maintenance and I've learned more about the jet than I did as a crew chief, because I'm gaining expertise from the different shops."

gave us a two-week pause to swap the jets. Then we had to train those students in the Block 42 jet, which is not vastly different, but some emergency procedures have changed because it's another engine, so the jet responds differently. The students had about 69 hours in the Viper at that point, thus were not wildly experienced, so we had to devise an ad hoc training programme to get them spun up on the Block 42. We had no issues, no mishaps and finished them out on the course.

"The transition to Block 42 aircraft helped us synergise with the rest of the fighter group – up to that point, we were the only squadron flying with GE engines, so it was not possible to integrate, because we couldn't cross B Courses over because of the different engine. Now all three squadrons are operating Block 42 aircraft powered by GE engines. Today, four of our lines were flown by the 314th Fighter Squadron because there are running a senior course [see below] and needed to complete some air-to-ground rides. We had some open lines, so the 314th pilots took four of our lines to meet the requirement."

Despite the aircraft swap, the 8th FS fleet of aircraft is ageing, as Lieutenant Colonel Marshall explained: "They've been very well used and have a lot of hours on them. Our maintainers do a fantastic job giving us safe and reliable aircraft to accomplish our mission, and we generally have what we need. There's not much that hasn't been figured out about the F-16 nowadays. Occasionally, you get a new thing present itself or something we never thought was going to be a problem, but because the aircraft has flown 8,000+ hours it's a problem. We address it and it gets solved, generally with a good engineering solution.

"Generally, we fly two turns a day, but that's somewhat dependent on the demands of the syllabus in terms of whether we need an F-16D with an instructor in the rear cockpit or whether the students are flying F-16C aircraft by themselves. We tend to plan to fly about 100 sorties or so per week, but the weekly total ebbs and flows based on weather and the maintenance health of the aircraft. We graduate 70 to 100 initial qualification students every year and that's been the pace for a while.

"We usually have two initial qualification or B Courses running simultaneously. They usually overlap on academics and simulators as the students learn some of the initial stuff and then get spun up. In addition, we run between three and seven instructor pilot upgrade courses with one or two people, along with transition courses for pilots coming back to the F-16 or from another platform. Occasionally, usually in the spring, we run senior officer courses for colonels, and generals going to a command who need a quick refresh."

In 2022, personnel assigned to the 314th FS and the 314th AMU created a sortie generation model that enables jets to be turned quickly and safely by integrating with the 311th FS, which shares ramp space with the 314th FS. The construct allowed both squadrons to utilise the other squadron's planes. It compressed time between arrival and departure and allowed the flying window to be shortened. When the flying window is shortened, the jet can be worked on for longer. All three F-16 squadrons assigned to the 54th FG now use the construct to improve the flow process.

EMBRACING ACE

The B Course executed by the three F-16 squadrons in the 54th Fighter Group follows a traditional concept of operations in which F-16s take off from Holloman, fly their missions and recover to Holloman. That flight routine is followed throughout all phases of the seven month syllabus because that's what the students need. However, this flight routine is aligned with the so-called 'big base' concept. Under the agile combat employment (ACE) paradigm, operations are shifting from centralised bases to a network of smaller, dispersed locations.

Discussing the impact of ACE, Lieutenant Colonel Marshall said: "We talk about ACE from an academic standpoint, but a lot of the things that we do are too basic to go into what the combat air force does with the concept. One way that we execute a version of ACE is during the initial transition rides. Students on their second ride in the F-16 flew to Biggs Army Airfield in El Paso, Texas, turned the jets, then flew their next ride to another location, so their flights were not from the same place every time. Our ability to do that is limited on the B Course because of syllabus constraints and localities, and we're to bot get too complicated. We leave a lot of that training to the combat air force – we send them pilots who are ready to receive that training."

A maintainer performs an inspection of the engine nozzle of an F-16 after a high-power engine run with afterburner at Holloman AFB, New Mexico. USAF Airman 1st Class Michelle Ferrari

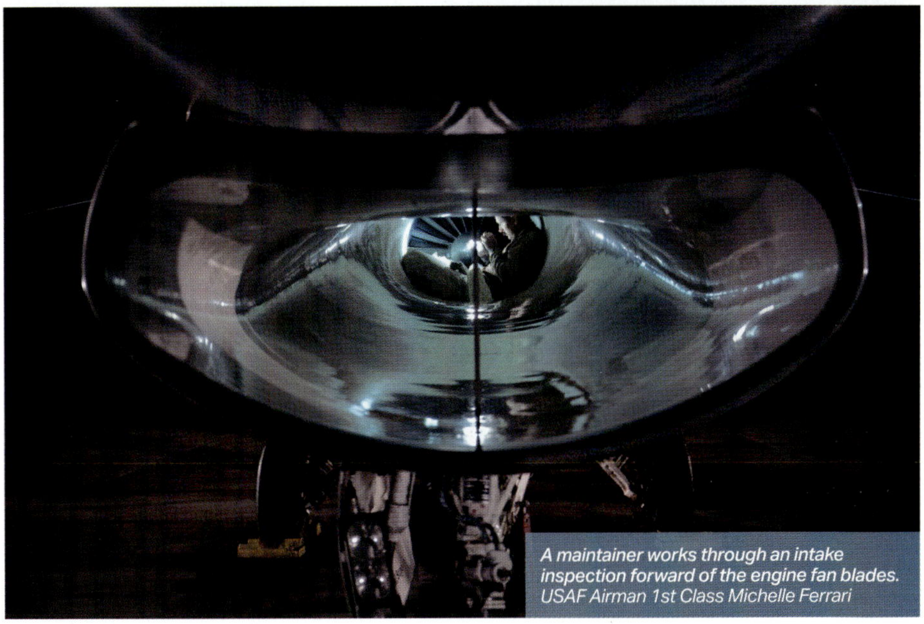

A maintainer works through an intake inspection forward of the engine fan blades. USAF Airman 1st Class Michelle Ferrari

MIG KILLER

On December 27, 1992, Lieutenant Colonel Gary North shot down an Iraqi Air Force MiG-25 *Foxbat*-E during a mission in support of Operation Southern Watch, flying Block 42 F-16D 90-0778 (c/n 1D-56). North was the first USAF pilot to score an air-to-air victory in an F-16 aircraft and the first pilot to make an air-to-air shootdown with an AIM-120 AMRAAM missile. Lieutenant Colonel North was the lead pilot of a flight of four F-16s assigned the 33rd Fighter Squadron home based at Shaw Air Force Base, South Carolina, at the time. The four F-16s were operating from Dharan Air Base, Saudi Arabia, deployed there in support of Operation Southern Watch.

The aircraft features a two-tone desert-style colour scheme, a black tail band containing the legend 'MiG Killer' and two green stars, with the title 'Operation Southern Watch' at the base of the tail, a green star containing a MiG-25 motif on the forward fuselage and the woridng 'Lt Col Gary 'Nordo' North' on the canopy rail.

The paintwork was completed by airmen assigned to the 56th Equipment Maintenance Squadron corrosion control team at Luke Air Force Base in June 2022. According to Sergeant Michael Cichonsky, a mechanic assigned to the 56th Equipment Maintenance Squadron, the colour scheme applied to aircraft 778 was based on the desert camouflage uniform worn by airmen at the time and a similar experimental camouflage tested on an F-16.

Aircraft 778 was inherited by the 8th Fighter Squadron at Holloman as part of the 2023 Block swap. The aircraft was originally delivered to Luke Air Force Base in July 1991.

MiG killer F-16D 90-778/HO on the 8th Fighter Squadron flight line at Holloman. It was flown by Lt Col Gary North when he shot down an Iraqi MiG-25 Foxbat *in December 1992. Mark Ayton*

MIG KILLER
HO
AF
90
778
OPERATION SOUTHERN WATCH

Jersey Devils

Atlantic City Air National Guard Base is home station of New Jersey ANG's 177th Fighter Wing equipped with F-16C Fighting Falcons.

Last summer, New Jersey ANG's 177th Fighter Wing (FW) flew some of its F-16s 7,000 miles to Komatsu Air Base, Japan, to participate in Exercise Resolute Force Pacific 2025 (REFORPAC), a first-of-its-kind department level exercise (DLE) designed to demonstrate the US armed services' ability to rapidly deploy personnel, equipment and aircraft to the Indo-Pacific theatre of operations.

Lieutenant Colonel Eric Emerson, 119th Expeditionary Fighter Squadron commander, explained: "REFORPAC will help solidify agile combat employment (ACE) concepts and execution among the men and women of the 177th FW. Lessons learned from this exercise will have a direct effect on how we train and fight. This exercise tests our ability to generate airpower with limited support and resources as we repositioned multiple times around Japan. We relied on airmen to step outside of their comfort zones, use their judgment backed up by their training while solving complex problems."

REFORPAC offered airmen an opportunity to work with service members of various US military branches as well as service members from other allied countries. Members of 177th FW had the opportunity to teach as well as learn different tactics, techniques and procedures, including refuelling aircraft, towing

F-16C 86-309/AC assigned to the 119th Fighter Squadron bearing the Jersey Jerk flagship tail flash at Atlantic City ANGB. The aircraft is dedicated to USAF Major General Donald Strait, a retired commander of the New Jersey ANG. US ANG/Senior Airman Darion Boyd

A crew chief with the 177th Fighter Wing prepares an F-16C at Boca Chica Field, Florida, during a training deployment. US ANG/SMSgt Andrew Moseley

A crew chief assigned to the 177th Fighter Wing verifies flight control surface checks on an F-16D Fighting Falcon, prior to launch at Boca Chica Field, Florida. US ANG/SMSgt Andrew Moseley

An F-16C from the 177th Fighter Wing after aerial refuelling with a KC-135R Stratotanker assigned to New Jersey ANG's 108th Wing en route to Naval Air Station Key West, Florida. US ANG/Senior Airman Hunter Hires

aircraft, providing equipment and training in emergency procedures for pilot extraction and hydrazine response.

HOME OF THE 'JERSEY DEVILS'

Located less than 150 miles south of New York City, Atlantic City International Airport in New Jersey is a busy commercial airport. The site also hosts the Atlantic City ANG Base, home to the 177th Fighter Wing part of New Jersey ANG. Equipped with Block 30 F-16C Fighting Falcons operated by the 119th Fighter Squadron, the 'Jersey Devils' traces its history to June 1917 and the 5th Aviation School Squadron. In October 1962, the 177th Tactical Fighter Group was activated with the 119th Tactical Fighter Squadron as its flying component. Subsequent re-designations were the 177th Fighter Interceptor Group in January 1973, the 177th Fighter Group in March 1992 and the 177th Fighter Wing in October 1995.

Lieutenant Colonel Michael Miles Long , commander of the 177th Operations Group and a seasoned F-16 pilot, commented: "We train for two main missions. One, overseas contingency operations, training for near-peer conflict in offensive counter air, close air support, surface attack and defensive counter air. Two, homeland defence, for which we stand an alert here at our home station, ready to go at a moment's notice. Our alert is tasked to defend down to South Carolina and up to New England. Our daily training revolves around the two mission sets, and each time we fly, we pick a specific mission and specific objectives, to maximise training in mission tailored to those two mindsets."

With concurrent alert tasking and general operations, 177th FW commanders must be cognizant of optimising the right people and the equipment to complete all its training objectives complete. Colonel Brian Cooper, the 177th Maintenance Group commander, explained: "From the maintenance group's perspective, that balance is felt every day. Prepping jets to go to the alert facility requires a more rigorous aircraft generation process. If an issue pops up on an alert aircraft, everything stops on the daily flying schedule to produce a replacement aircraft for the alert. We're constantly doing that around the clock, every day of the year to keep aircraft on alert status. Outside of such an incident, we must keep enough aircraft available on the flight line to meet the needs of the flight schedule every day, which generally comprises two turns.

"When I first joined this wing, on some days we were struggling to accomplish a two-turn-two schedule, mostly because of aircraft upgrades at the time and limitations with our critical maintainer career fields. Since then, we've changed our methods of risk acceptance and maintenance cultures in how we plan training. Consequently, we now consistently generate a six-turn-four schedule, which is impressive when compared to where we once were. Every week our pilots, maintainers, logistics and supply chain personnel meet for an hour to discuss aircraft availability and pilot currencies in detail, to ensure we're all operating from the same page. That gives us a full understanding of where we are as a wing, not just as ops or maintenance or supply, but collectively to make sure we can meet the next week's objectives."

All the wing's assigned F-16s are more than 35 years old, which makes it harder

OPERATION PEGASUS DAWN

Between October 18-25, 2024, the 119th Fighter Squadron deployed to Aviano Air Base, Italy, for Operation Pegasus Dawn, hosted by the 31st Fighter Wing. Pegasus Dawn was an ACE training mission designed to support the 108th Wing's transition from the KC-135R Stratotanker to the KC-46A Pegasus.

ACE is a proactive and reactive operational scheme of manoeuvres executed within threat timelines to increase survivability while generating combat air power. The strategy is executed by complicating the enemy's targeting process, creating political and operational dilemmas for the enemy and creating flexibility for friendly forces.

The purpose of Pegasus Dawn was to support the 108th Wing as their teams gained valuable experience with three KC-46 aircraft deployed to the US Air Forces in Europe theatre, while integrating the aircraft and airmen into their existing systems and areas of responsibility. Pilots with the 119th FS completed daily missions, to provide relevant ACE experience for the new tanker crews, primarily as receivers to ensure the basic aerial refuelling systems were operational.

Major Timothy Mann, F-16 pilot and director of flying with the 119th FS, said: "We received fuel from them on the transatlantic flight and conducted aerial refuelling with them each day of this deployment. We conducted a mix of offensive counter air and defensive counter air missions with the 108th Wing and additional F-16s from the 555th Fighter Squadron based at Aviano."

Crew chiefs assigned to the 177th Aircraft Maintenance Squadron (AMXS) serviced the F-16s and undertook maintenance activities outside of their typical air force specialty code. Lieutenant Colonel Jessica Lewis, 177th AMXS commander, explained: "We had structural shop airmen assisting with replacing liquid oxygen and marshalling jets, and engine shop airmen assisting with tyre changes. We're performing aircraft maintenance with a smaller footprint, which increases our flexibility for any future fight to come."

Major Mann added: "This week's partnership proves that the flying units of the New Jersey ANG can operate almost autonomously. It shows that our state and its airmen can organically deploy personnel, equipment and airpower around the world with little to no outside support."

An F-16C Fighting Falcon from the 177th Fighter Wing receives fuel from a KC-135R Stratotanker assigned to New Jersey ANG's 108th Wing. US ANG/Senior Airman Hunter Hires

for the 177th Maintenance Group to get parts. That's not unique to the F-16 because every aircraft type has challenges with parts supply. The solution depends on the strength of the air force supply chain system, but cannibalising parts or using suitable substitutions are two alternative options for sourcing unavailable parts.

DEPLOYMENT

In the days when the 177th was gained by and assigned to Aerospace Defense Command and solely tasked with the defence of the United States, the wing made no overseas deployments. After the Aerospace Defense Command was inactivated, the 177th's gaining command became Tactical Air Command and, by 1994, the wing re-equipped with Block 25 F-16s with multi-role capability. This changed the wing's ability to deploy and it has been regularly tasked with overseas missions ever since.

Most recently, the 177th FW deployed to the US Central Command AOR in 2021, participating in Air Combat Command's Combat Archer air-to-air weapon systems evaluation programme at Tyndall Air Force Base, Florida, and Exercise Red Flag at Nellis Air Force Base, Nevada, in March 2023. The 'Jersey Devils' returned to the US Central Command AOR in 2023, capping off a busy year for an ANG unit with a lot of part-time guardsmen in addition to standing alert. Commenting, Lieutenant Colonel Miles said: "It was a heavy lift for us, but in true 'Jersey Devils' spirit, we got the job done."

Last October, the 177th FW deployed to Aviano Air Base, Italy, for an ACE training event called Operation Pegasus Dawn. Outlining the event, Lieutenant Colonel Miles said: "Our sister unit, the 108th Wing based at McGuire Air Force Base is transitioning to the KC-46, so the deployment to Aviano provided an opportunity to drag fighters across the ocean, complete training overseas and then redeploy home. Initially, it started as a support commitment to the 108th Wing, but we always want to get training accomplished. We focused

F-16C 87-265/AC takes off from Atlantic City ANG Base. US ANG/Senior Airman Hunter Hires

on manning the deployment to Aviano with the smallest footprint we could take, having sufficient people and maintenance equipment to be able to operate and sustain fighter operations for several days at an overseas base. That was our overarching objective. We also completed a lot of upgrade training for the maintainers and the pilots while flying with F-16s assigned to the 31st Fighter Wing. We stopped at RAF Mildenhall in the UK on the return trip home. Stayed there for one night and continued home to New Jersey the following day."

Rounding up the discussion about the ACE paradigm, Colonel Cooper said: "We believe wholeheartedly in the ACE concept but there are risks that we take into a combat environment, which are not the same risks that

A maintainer marshals an F-16C during Operation Pegasus Dawn at Aviano Air Base, Italy, on October 22, 2024. US ANG/Senior Airman Darion Boyd

F-16C 87-346/AC seen on the taxiway at an air base in the US Central Command's area of responsibility. US ANG

The tail of the flagship F-16C 86-309/AC assigned to the 119th Fighter Squadron bearing the Jersey Jerk tail flash. US ANG/Senior Airman Darion Boyd

we accept on a day-to-day training operation. So we continue to train our young airmen and pilots and maintainers to be able to identify the risks that could potentially happen in a combat scenario, while trying to build the ACE concept as a mindset in all day-to-day training."

COMBAT ARCHER

In January 2023, the 'Jersey Devils' deployed to Tyndall Air Force Base, Florida, to participate in Air Combat Command's Combat Archer air-to-air weapons system evaluation programme (WSEP). Pilots, maintainers and support staff launched and recovered 150 sorties during the training which tests and evaluates multiple areas of operations, including weapons loading, missile employment and aerial gunnery.

Lieutenant Colonel Long, commander of the 119th Fighter Squadron, explained: "One of the training goals is to familiarise the pilot to weapons deployment in combat, something that very few pilots experience more than once in their career. One of the aspects that makes Combat Archer unique is that pilots can employ live weapons, preparing them for that feeling of the missile or bomb coming off the jet."

Commenting on Combat Archer, Colonel Cooper said: "Because of our alert mission, we always have aircraft loaded with live missiles, so our folks are pretty adept at loading 'lives' on aircraft. Combat Archer ensures that maintainers can load the weapons correctly, and for pilots, WSEP builds confidence that the aircraft will operate as it should, the missile station communicates with the aircraft and the missile will come off the launch rail as it should. It also provides an opportunity for a pilot to put their understanding of tactics, techniques and procedures in to practise with a live-fire shot. It's a pretty big deal. Ten mostly young pilots shot missiles – we usually prioritise pilots who have never shot missiles before.

"We pride ourselves on our maintenance and we had a 99.9% success rate in all the categories evaluated, which takes dozens of maintainers to make happen. Combat Archer is invaluable training to us. When the maintainers watch the aircraft come back with nothing on the rail, that's a really great experience for them. One cool tradition we follow is to allow the maintainers to keep the missile release rings.

"The WSEP programme is essentially mandatory for all air force fighter squadrons, with some wiggle room, but we don't control our participation."

Discussing the training requirements in preparation for a deployment, Lieutenant Colonel Long said: "There are all kinds of training requirements for each deployment location, for the mission and for individuals. Everybody has specific training to be combat ready. Participation in a WSEP, Red, Green or Silver Flag are training exercises that enable us to be considered ready for combat. We conduct spin-up training ahead of whichever exercise we're tasked to attend."

CENTCOM DEPLOYMENT

During its last deployment to the CENTCOM AOR, the 119th Expeditionary Fighter Squadron completed a no-notice real-world combat ACE. Lieutenant Colonel Long explained: "We had less than 24 hours from notification to execution, which was complicated because the aircraft we had to move were not at the main operating base. So, in 24 hours, we had to recover aircraft to the main operating base, where our maintainers took about three hours to drop some stores and load missiles, bombs, bullets and prep the aircraft to complete an ACE mission. Pilots then flew to an alternate location and stood up combat ops within 22 hours of notification. At the forward location our pilots launched and recovered each other on combat missions because our maintainers were still en route. There were a lot of moving pieces, but we did the job extremely well.

"We had six pilots at the forward base who launched each other using a system where two pilots would sleep, while other pilots would recover those airplanes and refuel them, check the oil and the hydraulics. We weren't launching all the planes at once, so we always had extra pilots on hand to launch, recover and then check the fluids. But you can only do that for two days, so we needed the maintainers to get to the forward base. Once they arrived, they worked for 12 hours straight to keep the aircraft flying on real combat missions."

In 2021, Colonel Cooper had helped close-down Bagram Air Base in Afghanistan and was one of the last groups of air force personnel to get out of the country: "Our fighter squadron, the 119th Expeditionary Fighter Squadron, was deployed to Bagram

New Jersey ANG's 119th Expeditionary Fighter Squadron arrives in the US Central Command's area of responsibility in late 2023. US ANG

F-16C 87-225/AC, undergoes final checks at the end of runway ramp at Komatsu Air Base, Japan, during Exercise Resolute Force Pacific 2025. US ANG/Senior Airman Darion Boyd

and was the last to leave. When the full evacuation order came for Afghanistan, people and aircraft were deploying to other bases. Our fighter squadron's F-16s, pilots and maintainers were scheduled to go to another location outside of Afghanistan. I volunteered to help close the base down. The task needed skilled people, so asked some of the maintainers and munitions people to stay to help close-down the base, which primarily involved moving things."

JERSEY JERK

F-16C 86-309 assigned to the 119th Fighter Squadron is painted with a coloured tail and wears the name Jersey Jerk **in honour to Major General Donald Strait, a New Jersey ANG ace who initially served as a P-47N Thunderbolt pilot with the 356th Fighter Group in World War Two. At the time, Strait named his P-47N aircraft** Jersey Jerk**. He had wanted to use** Jersey Bounce**, but that name was already taken. Reluctant to include the word 'Jerk' in the name of his plane, he relented after his crew chief told him: "Sir, let me tell you why we want to name it that. Any guy that would take off in a single engine airplane, cross the North Sea in the wintertime and take a chance of getting his ass shot off by the Luftwaffe or by anti-aircraft fire has got to be a jerk." Strait went on to command the 'Jersey Devils' and became the commander of the entire New Jersey ANG, retiring as a two-star general.**

A US Marine based at Marine Corps Air Station, Iwakuni, Japan, assists an airman assigned to the 177th Fighter Wing during forward area refuelling point operations at Komatsu Air Base, Japan, during Exercise Resolute Force Pacific 2025. US ANG/Senior Airman Darion Boyd

OPERATION BELT FEED

Airmen assigned to the 177th Fighter Wing participated in a training exercise called Operation Belt Feed at Fort Drum, New York, on June 24, 2025. The exercise tested the airmen's ability to rapidly deploy combat airpower with limited knowledge of mission details. Airmen who participated in the exercise were given minimal information until they arrived at Fort Drum aboard a C-130H Hercules assigned to the Delaware ANG.

Explaining Belt Feed, Lieutenant Colonel Long said: "As an air arme, we put a lot of emphasis on these large-scale events like Flags and WSEPs. They serve a purpose, but they're mostly geared towards the operators. They don't normally allow our airmen to explore the space, think on their feet, truly make risk-assessments or enhance the agile mindset we absolutely need."

During Belt Feed, two 119th Fighter Squadron F-16s landed, taxied to a parking spot for refuelling and reloading of weapons and took off again. The scope of future exercises will seek to strengthen the lethality and readiness of airmen assigned to the 177th Fighter Wing.

Pitch Rocking

More than 35 years in the F-16 test business, the 416th Flight Test Squadron based at Edwards Air Force Base, California, undertakes some cool stuff.

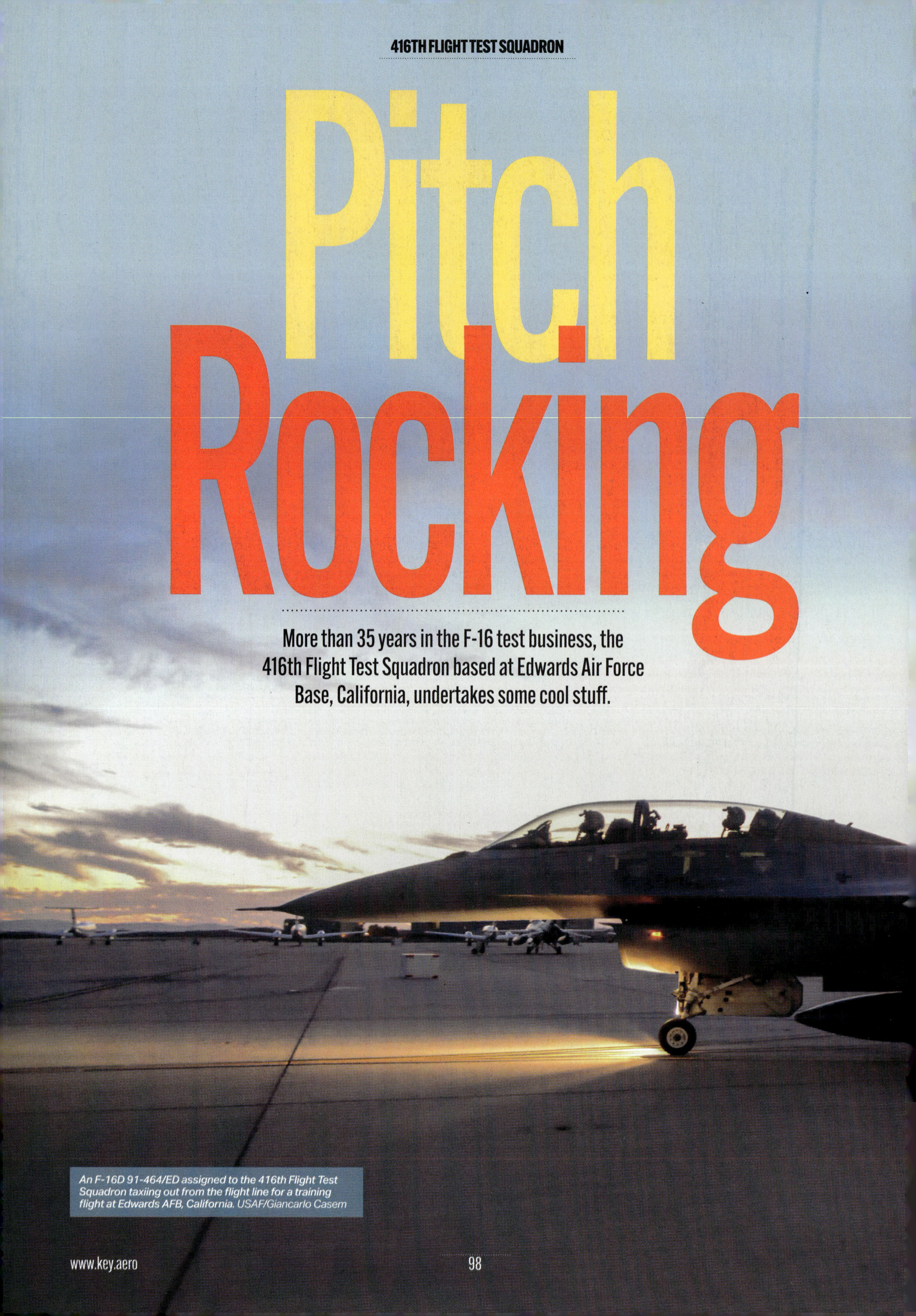

An F-16D 91-464/ED assigned to the 416th Flight Test Squadron taxiing out from the flight line for a training flight at Edwards AFB, California. USAF/Giancarlo Casem

The 416th Flight Test Squadron (FLTS) is one of two USAF F-16 developmental test units that undertake flight testing of software, hardware, stores and munitions for the USAF and allied nations that operate the Fighting Falcon. The second unit is the 40th FLTS based at Eglin Air Force Base, Florida, (see *Fighting Fortieth*, p62). The squadron's nickname is the 'Skulls'.

Its primary mission sets are F-16 flight tests and providing test support to other programmes across the 412th Test Wing with its aircraft, pilots, flight test engineers and discipline engineers. Leading these efforts is Major Thomas Ainscough, an F-16 test pilot and director of operations with the 416th FLTS, who oversees the training, qualification and proficiency of squadron test pilots and aircrew, including aerial photographers. Major Ainscough also undertakes planning for upcoming flight test programmes and writes test reports outlining the results.

Flight test planning involves the organisation and allocation of resources, developing good test methodology with discipline engineers and documentation of flight test plans. In general, a flight test plan includes details of the purpose and scope of the test, the number of flights required to accomplish each objective, the duration of each flight, the flight path and manoeuvres, the test point criteria, test configurations and conditions, the techniques for risk reduction and data measurements, rate and format type.

One of the unit's primary tasks is development the latest operational flight programme (OFP) software to continue the ongoing upgrade process of the F-16 weapon system, to make sure the aircraft remains lethal, effective and able to meet the demands of the modern battlespace. The latest OFP is dubbed M8.26.

Explaining one current programme, Major Ainscough said: "We're expanding the F-16's computing power to enable the aircraft to run mission systems with advanced capabilities that produce a lot more data. Two such mission systems are the APG-83 AESA radar, which provides a much greater capability to find, track, detect and engage a variety of targets at different distances, and the ALQ-254 Viper Shield electronic warfare system, which increases the ability to find and engage targets at different ranges.

"Some of the less exciting work is the verification of the rehosting of current OFPs run on the new computer, making sure it still functions. This is known as regression testing – making sure we haven't broken anything in the existing weapon system as we move things around to make room to process all the additional data. In addition, we test the new mission systems and their capabilities to ensure those are all working.

"If we load a new munition which is significantly different to existing weapons and might affect the handling characteristics and departure resistance of the F-16, we perform flying qualities testing. Issues with the aircraft's flying qualities may affect avionics systems, such as the auto Ground Collision Avoidance System (GCAS), which was originally tested by the 416th FLTS at Edwards in 2011. We continue to update, refine and increase the capabilities of the auto GCAS and undertake flying qualities testing in support of that.

"Much of our ongoing flying qualities testing is undertaken to expand the F-16's flight envelope for foreign military sale (FMS) programmes in support of allies who have requirements for their F-16s that differ from USAF F-16s. For example, a country that may not have ready access to aerial refuelling wants to fly with 600-gallon external fuel tanks to add range and endurance. We've completed a lot of envelope expansion with such tanks compared to the standard USAF 370-gallon tank. The 600-gallon tanks have a destabilising

A 416th Flight Test Squadron F-16 loaded with a captive carriage version of the Norwegian joint strike missile. USAF/Christian Turner

The crew of an F-16 assigned to the 416th Flight Test Squadron works through pre-flight checks for a night training flight at Edwards AFB, California. USAF/Giancarlo Casem

effect on the aircraft and some of its flight characteristics. We're clearing the envelope and making sure that flight control law updates compensate for the effects of the larger tanks and that the aircraft still meets the mission requirements and handles appropriately."

Most of the recent munition testing undertaken by the 416th FLTS was for international partners. Captain Alexander Brown, lead F-16 flight test engineer, explained: "Different countries want to integrate different weapons on their F-16s. In support of FMS customers, the 416th tests the avionics, safe weapons separation, environmental testing [to verify that the physical integrity of an item under test will survive the intended flight environment], handling qualities [to evaluate the aircraft's response to a disturbance or flight control input throughout the range of flight to determine stability and control characteristics], structural testing [to verify the integrity of the aircraft or a system for both air-to-ground and air-to-air weapons."

BLOCK 70 FLIGHT TESTING

Edwards Air Force Base made no secret of the arrival of the first Block 70 F-16 at the Californian base on March 28, 2023. The aircraft involved was Royal Bahrain Air Force F-16D 1611 (c/n EB-1). The Bahraini jet is assigned to the 416th FLTS and led the ongoing Block 70 flight test programme. The 416th also operates a second Bahraini Block 70 aircraft, F-16C 1601 (c/n EA-1).

Without reference to a specific country, giving some details of the test activities conducted with Block 70 F-16s to date, Major Ainscough said: "The Block 70 F-16 has a lot of significant upgrades and the most significant testing we're doing right now is a brand-new flight control computer called CD/2, which adds in significant capabilities for the F-16,including enhancing the safety of the pilot. One capability prevents the aircraft from going into a departure, beyond the stall to the point where the aircraft departs controlled flight and is no longer flying. There are functions designed to augment the existing flight control systems to prevent that from happening in the first place. That said, the F-16 has a unique condition due to its aerodynamics and its relaxed static stability that, when it departs, it can end up in what's called a deep stall. So the aircraft can end up in a stable position of about 60° angle of attack. If it gets stuck in that position, it may not recover and requires pilot action. With the previous Blocks, the pilot had to apply the necessary procedures to manually recover the aircraft through a technique called 'pitch rocking'. With the Block 70 and CD/2, the flight control computer can detect that departure, detect the deep stall condition in both upright and inverted conditions and recover the aircraft on its own.

"High angle of attack departure testing is something with which Edwards has a lot of experience, and we've been conducting it in the F-16 for decades. One significant sub-objective of high angle of attack departure testing is providing training to pilots from both the USAF and international partners. Pilots come to the 416th and we give them a chance to fly manoeuvres that are prohibited in the flight manual – the pilots intentionally put the aircraft into a deep stall to train how to recover the aircraft and save lives.

"Block 30 F-16s and prior are referred to as the system capability upgrade (SCU) variants, while Block 40 and on, are referred to as modular mission computer (MMC) variants. Lockheed Martin has separately developed the Viper upgrade, the standard configuration for all FMS partners, its predominantly avionics-centric and like the advanced USAF avionics configuration. The aircraft come from all different Blocks. We operate Block 20 aircraft with the Viper upgrade, featuring modern avionics but a legacy analogue flight control computer. We've tested those aircraft with additional capabilities, such as a hybrid flight control computer (HFLCC) to provide additional safety and resiliency built into an aircraft equipped with analogue flight control procedures."

Air Force Research Laboratory engineers developed the HFLCC, which enables integration of digital cards into F-16 analogue flight control computers. This allows F-16s that are not equipped with digital flight control computers to incorporate collision avoidance technology. The HFLCC programme, directed by the F-16 system programme office (SPO), is one of the biggest recently undertaken by the 416th FLTS.

FLIGHT TEST ENGINEER

Captain Brown explained that the role of a flight test engineer "is one of co-ordination between test pilots, aircrew, maintainers and all the engineers involved in a test programme, to get everything organised to execute testing. Flight test engineers are multi-skilled and hold specialist qualifications for departure flights or structures, tests that have safety concerns, but generally we're responsible for the whole system. We operate in control rooms for many of the squadron's flight test events, especially those that are high-risk, or take place near the edge of the envelope."

Much of Captain Brown's job involves scheduling the flight test engineers to ensure all test programmes are supported week to week, in conjunction with the pilot scheduling officed: "We must be experts on the systems

A crew chief and a test pilot work through pre-flight checks for a flight test of a Gray Wolf captive carriage cruise missile prototype at Edwards AFB, California. USAF/Kyle Brazier

under test, to ensure any request received from the SPO is executable here at Edwards, that we have the resources and equipment required and meet the test requirements, so that, ultimately, we provide the maximum capability to the operational wings and squadrons.

"We also have a lot of input in the test cards [a flight test card outlines the sequence of events in which to conduct the test and details the test aircraft's identification, the test objective, a description of the aircraft's configuration and that of the test point, manoeuvres and acceptance criteria]. We're involved in the test process from start to finish. The SPO issues the requirements and details the things they want to test. We look through the request to ensure the testing can be accomplished at Edwards. That involves creating a test plan, which is signed off by the 416th FLTS managers and the 412th Operations Group. Then we create a safety plan to ensure we've considered everything that could possibly go wrong, with a contingency to make sure those things don't happen and have procedures in place in case something does.

"We work with our discipline engineers – experts in their field, for example avionics, radar or flying qualities – to create the test cards with all the information, making sure they're easy to read and are executable by our pilots and aircrew. I'm a non-rated aircrew able to fly as a flight test engineer at Edwards with the ability to lead and execute tests from the aft cockpit to help aid the pilot with some of the workload that's not specifically related to controlling the aircraft. The 416th has more two-seat F-16D aircraft assigned than an operational unit would typically have, so we can support specific flight test missions.

"Flying in the aft seat helps us perform our job better by knowing what the environment is like, knowing what the pilots and the aircraft can do, all of which helps us to make

416th Flight Test Squadron F-16D 87-392/ED on a photo chase mission at Edwards AFB, California. USAF/Todd Schannuth

good decisions early in the development of a test programme. Flight test engineers are the bridge between the pilot and the discipline engineers, those individuals that know everything about a particular system, but not necessarily about how that relates to operations, or the F-16 flight environment. The discipline engineer may look at their graphs and charts and request the pilot to hold a constant 6G turn at exactly Mach 0.8, at a specific altitude, while managing something that's difficult to execute. The flight test engineer helps set-up the test to get the data required by the discipline engineer in a way that a pilot can safely and effectively execute."

Flight test engineers occasionally operate specific and unique test equipment, when for example, testing a different pod or to support another programme as the subject matter expert operating the piece of equipment while the pilot is flying the aircraft.

PRODUCING AIRCRAFT FOR TEST FLIGHTS

MSgt Benjamin Benefield is a production superintendent with the 412th Aircraft Maintenance Squadron. Leading a production team is a busy and complex task. His team undertake a complicated schedule of maintenance to ensure that multiple stakeholders get a chance to fly their test missions.

Discussing the role, Benefield said: "I must balance mission requirement with maintenance scheduling. Different jets require different amounts of maintenance at different times. I must do all that with a large group of young men and women who, but for technical school, are not long out of high school. We ask them to come to the middle of the California desert to train, work and become subject

matter experts on every variation of the F-16 that exists in the USAF inventory, including foreign military sale aircraft. Block 25s, 30s, 40s, 50s, hybrids… no two jets are the same. Each one is modified to a different extent, with different instrumentation for different test parameters.

"We expect our team to know enough to be able to put a safe and reliable aircraft in the air or have the wherewithal to tell me when they don't think it's safe: that's a lot of responsibility to put on young people. We have civilians, Lockheed Martin people and those from other agencies that work with us. The civilians certainly fill an experience gap left when an experienced airman moves to their next assignment. That loss of experience can't be the reason that a test flight doesn't go up.

"The average age of our planes is 30+ years old. Trying to get the equipment and parts we need to fix them is becoming exceedingly difficult. Air frames are getting old and tired. Different jets have different personalities, and you need to know which jets need more attention. Different tests require different configurations. When you're at an installation like Shaw, every jet you have is the same, so it's easy, from a production standpoint, to adjust and compensate for whatever the mission demands. At Edwards that's not the case. I never thought I would have to tell majors and colonels: "No, you can't have an F-16 to fly." Yes, it might be the only D-model of that variant, with that modification, but you

Royal Bahrain Air Force Block 70 F-16D 1611 (c/n EB-1) over Edwards AFB, California on its delivery flight from South Carolina on March 28, 2023. USAF/412th Test Wing

can't have that jet because another mission has a higher priority. Or conversely, I must tell them no, because of logistics, if you break my plane, I can't fix it. I can't get parts. I don't have the resources. And that would affect other test missions down the line."

The 416th's fleet of F-16s are fitted with flight test instrumentation and telemetry systems, any of which affect the maintenance of the aircraft: "It depends on the age of the instrumentation, who did the modification and how it's tapped into the aircraft's different systems. If you like solving puzzles, troubleshooting avionic systems is an absolute blast. You'll be following a wiring diagram, trying to figure out why a signal isn't getting from point A to point B. The wiring diagram will tell you that there's instrumentation tapped in, but our contractors will tell us there's nothing there. However, you remember that years ago someone did tap in instrumentation, meaning there's a broken tie point somewhere that you must find. That's a lot of wires to go through to isolate."

One Block 50 F-16C assigned to the 416th FLTS has a spin-chute installed which affects the pre-flight processes involved with preparing the aircraft for a test mission. A Block 50 aircraft fitted with a spin chute is heavily modified. The original flight control computer has been removed and replaced by a new device. Additionally, one of the multifunction displays is used to control the spin chute. Benefield explained: "If the spin chute is installed and the aircraft is being prepared for a departure test, we tow the aircraft to a pad and conduct the pre-flight procedures there. This is a safety precaution so that if the chute unexpectedly deploys it doesn't take out everyone around it. For the test flight we may have to change certain software, swap out the stores to configure the aircraft either symmetrically or asymmetrically, and set up the jet to meet the test requirements. Most importantly, we need to establish if they want the aircraft to depart controlled flight or not?

"We are in constant communication with the pilots, flight test engineers and maintainers when preparing for a flight test event. There's nothing that we can do on the jet without talking to maintenance to make sure they're able to support and have the jet in its right configuration for the test. If I mess something up and I tell them something is wrong, the aircraft is not going to go. If I tell them to do something and then something needs to be done for a test and they do it wrong, the aircraft is not going to go. If the pilot doesn't know what to expect from the test and is not prepared, it puts the aircrew at risk, so the aircrew are involved from the start to make sure that anything we do is ultimately safe, and they are comfortable and know exactly what to expect when they get in the aircraft.

"Money can solve a lot of issues, but experience is not one of them. There is so much groundwork that goes into making any test happen. If they want to change the software and the MMC, that takes a full eight-hour shift of just reloading software. Then there's all the second and third order effects to make sure the MMC is correctly configured, and because the software changed, it's changed other things that you must correct and if any system doesn't take the software when it's supposed to, you troubleshoot it.

"Here's an example, if we're given the wrong software load and we load it on the aircraft, that

Royal Bahrain Air Force F-16D 1611 (c/n EB-1) touches down at Edwards AFB, California, on March 28, 2023, with full national insignia and tail markings. USAF/412th Test Wing

RBAF
1611
18-0011

LOCKHEED MARTIN LEGION-ES IRST

The Legion-ES (Embedded System) is a brand-new variant of the IRST21 (Infrared Search and Track) sensor suite used by other types, but is a new capability for the F-16.

The system's processor is installed internally and the sensor head is housed in a pod carried on the inlet's station 5L opposite the targeting pod. Based on its size, the sensor head could not sensibly be fitted on the fuselage anywhere it made sense. Because Lockheed Martin had already cleared certain stores for carriage on station 5L, integration of the Legion-ES pod was less expensive and complied with the USAF Seek Eagle certification process. The Seek Eagle certification process determines safe and acceptable carriage and release limits, loading and unloading procedures, safe escape parameters and ballistic accuracy for weapons fitted to USAF and foreign military sales aircraft. Stores compatibility is aided by modelling, analysis, and scientific and engineering methodologies.

According to Lockheed Martin Missiles and Fire Control, Legion-ES provides long-range detection and tracking capability of airborne threats with weapon-quality accuracy, a low false alarm rate and a large field of regard while staying immune to electronic deception and attack by adversaries. Legion-ES is complementary to other on-board and off-board aircraft sensors, enabling multispectral engagement.

The Legion-ES weighs less than 300lb, measures 77in in length, has a 9.75in diameter and requires two-level maintenance.

eats up an entire 24 hours. We lose not just that test line, but we also lose a test line we could have had on the schedule the following week, because the lost line has to be moved to make up for the gap that we just put into it. It's a house of cards that you must balance, which is why, in maintenance and production, we're prudent with how we allow different organisations access to our planes to the best of our ability.

"The aircraft fitted with a spin chute is a one-of-a-kind asset we're using to enable the testing of the future capabilities of the Block 70. When scheduling that aircraft, we know it's the specific tail we need to execute the test with the spin chute installed. Our flight test engineer works for months in advance to determine what other testing might also need that F-16. Or can we move the testing scheduled on that aircraft to a different aircraft and then co-ordinate with maintenance to make sure the specific instrumentation is installed and working, and which test boxes might need to be swapped out?

F-16C 88-456 assigned to the 416th Flight Test Squadron with a 50th Anniversary Fighting Falcon tail flash flies over the desert of Southern California. USAF/Todd Schannuth

F-16C 88-456 flies over California's Sierra Nevada mountains. USAF/Todd Schannuth

"Once a flight test is complete, there's a lot of follow-ups co-ordinating with maintenance on any anomalies that we saw, what things worked well. Did anything unexpected happen, did anything not go according to our expected results? Then we work with the engineers to make sure we gathered the data we need and, if we didn't, why and how we can correct it, to ensure the overall test programme keeps moving forward."

THE LONG ROAD TO TESTING

Some test events take a year or more to develop and implement the safe execution of the test, especially if it will be flown on the edges of the aircraft's flight envelope. According to Captain Brown: "There might be specific resources or configuration changes required on the jet – for example, for loads testing, we might want to limit the amount of G we can pull, to prevent the airplane being flown beyond its limits. That helps the pilot keep the aircraft within a controlled configuration and not overstrain the structure. We plan with maintenance for the different modifications that are required and decide exactly where they can fit on an aircraft, especially for anything new or that might present a safety concern."

On any given day, Captain Brown works concurrently on multiple different test programmes scheduled for that week, next week, in a month and sometimes in a year's time. Providing his take on the long lead-in to a test, MSgt Benefield said: "When planning things years out, there are so many layers of constraint to make the test happen. When they select a plane, production must balance phase flow, maintenance, changes to the aircraft… there's so much that can happen. For example, does the jet have to fly more or fly less hours? Has it got to be modified with the equipment and the wiring to make the test happen? All such work rides on the back of graduates fresh out of tech school."

Providing a test pilot's input, Major Ainscough said: "As the pilot of a single-seat aircraft, you're just one person in a team of hundreds of people, whether it's a large group of maintainers that prepped the aircraft and got it ready with all the unique modifications needed, or flight test engineers or discipline engineers who monitored one specific parameter of a particular flight control or air speed to ensure safety of flight, so that we can execute the higher risk, complex test events safely and effectively."

Major Ainscough highlighted how much the F-16 has evolved from where it started 50 years ago: "As the threat environment continues to be more complex, the F-16 remains relevant and will continue to be so for decades. That's due to the capabilities it has, the large number in operation, and the wide variety of missions it can perform. The 416th FLTS continues to ensure it still has its teeth and will continue to be an effective

F-16C 88-456 uploads fuel from a KC-135 tanker over the desert of Southern California. USAF/Todd Schannuth

part of the overall joint fight for many years to come. Much of our work is focused on the Block 70 variants, because it affects a lot of different countries as production continues to move forward."

BLOCK 70

On January 24, 2023, Lockheed Martin test pilots Dwayne Opella and Monessa Balzhiser took off from Donaldson Center Airport, Greenville, South Carolina in F-16D 1611 (c/n EB-1) on the maiden flight of the brand-new Block 70 variant. The 50-minute flight included airworthiness checks of the GE Aerospace F110-GE-129D engine, flight controls, the fuel system and aircraft handling. EB-1 is the first of ten F-16Cs and six F-16Ds on order by the variant's launch customer, the Royal Bahraini Air Force.

The aircraft flew from Greenville to Edwards Air Force Base, California, on March 28 for an independent flight test programme conducted by the USAF. Aircraft EB-1 was being used by the 416th FLTS to test the aircraft's V3 OFP software and the Viper Shield electronic warfare system.

As part of its development effort for the Block 70 F-16, Lockheed Martin made improvements to the structure of the aircraft and increased its service life by 50% from 8,000 to 12,000 hours. As foreign military sale items, Block 70 and Block 72 aircraft are designated F-16C and F-16D, as controlled by the USAF. For clarity, a Block 70 F-16 is powered by the GE Aerospace F110-GE-129D and a Block 72 by the Pratt & Whitney F100-PW-229EEP.

The Block 70 has a larger inlet duct, dubbed the big mouth inlet, and the Block 72 has a

standard size shock inlet. Because the engine variant dictates the type of inlet, at the time of contract signature, the customer's choice of engine is critical to allow Lockheed Martin to build the correct inlet on the jet. The customer selects their choice of engine and the engine units are purchased by the US government.

The Block 70 is equipped with what Lockheed Martin calls the upgraded Viper avionics package. This includes a new flight control computer called the Common Digital Flight Control Computer 2 which, unsurprisingly, is more capable than the legacy flight control computer developed for Block 40 F-16s. The new computer has more memory, more processing or throughput capability and is coupled to the autopilot, auto throttle and the automatic ground collision avoidance system (GCAS). All three auto-systems and a deep stall recovery function help improve flight safety. In simple terms, the new computer can do more things, not least make missions easier for the pilot even before take-off. The mission plan can be completed in the squadron's planning cell, uploaded to a cartridge and inserted into a dock on the aircraft for upload to the new computer. Once airborne, the aircraft can fly to a series of way points at the altitude and speed required by the pilot.

The new F-16 is equipped with what Lockheed Martin calls an advanced cockpit with a bunch of upgraded features. These include electronic gauges for the engine, fuel and electronic utility, each with hot lines wired in. If a gauge detects an out of tolerance reading, a red advisory light is displayed to the pilot. The fuel gauge feeds the capacity of each tank instantaneously, so the pilot can see how much fuel is in each without having to call the information up on the display.

To make the cockpit more user friendly for the pilot, Lockheed Martin has rearranged the switches and installed a digital intercom system with 3-D audio. This cancels engine

Royal Bahraini Air Force F-16D 1611 (c/n EB-1) flies behind a KC-135 tanker during a mission from Edwards AFB. USAF/Richard Gonzales

noise and features a capability known as spatial separation. This enables the pilot to discern who is talking on the radio – either the weapon systems officer in the aft cockpit or crew from accompanying aircraft.

The all-important centre pedestal has been upgraded and features a 6in x 8in display and changes to some of the controls. According to Mike McSpadden, Lockheed Martin's F-16 chief engineer, the company considered using a large area display in the F-16, as per the F-35 – a big undertaking that it opted not to carry-through.

For completeness, a 4in x 4in display is positioned on each side of the centre pedestal at the top. The 6in x 8in display is fed digital imagery from the targeting pod via a new digital video interface and the upfront control panel that's used for data entry has been moved to facilitate more buttons necessitated by the new common digital flight control computer. Lockheed Martin also added a new stand-by flight instrument which is equipped with a gauge to ensure critical flight information is always displayed to the pilot.

Explaining how the head-up display (HUD) remained unchanged with the same functionality, Mike McSpadden said: "When we considered a large area display, there was talk about getting rid of the HUD, but all the test pilots liked the HUD, so we didn't change."

Explaining the display, McSpadden said: "There is some display fusion for the pilot. It's like the F-35 system, but it's not the same. All sensors feed to the display, AIFF, radar, EW and targeting pod, and most of the information can be switched between the three displays. The pilot has the option to switch whatever data he wants on which displays he is focused on. The pilot can customise what he sees, he can zoom in, zoom out, have a colour moving map on the display, different backgrounds and can place something on the top two thirds and something different on the bottom third." McSpadden was unable to discuss the fusion aspect any further due to its restricted nature.

The new F-16 is equipped with two dual-band UHF/VHF radios as standard, each with new security features. Additional radios can be installed to meet specific customer requirements.

The new F-16D has independent crew stations front and aft, enabling the aft unit to be used as a weapon system officer station. This is a new set-up – on a legacy F-16D, the aft crew station was a repeater station to the front; the pilot in the front crew station selected what he needed/wanted to look at and the weapon system officer in the aft crew station saw the same thing. In the new F-16D, the weapon system officer has complete control on what they see on their displays. Given that there is no means to provide an independent HUD for the aft crew, the HUD is a repeater of the front crew station. Beyond that there are no systems that can only be operated in the aft cockpit.

As with earlier Block aircraft, the Block 70 F-16D is fully combat-capable with the same abilities as a single-seat F-16C and a pilot in the aft crew station can fly and land the aircraft.

NEW RADAR

The new F-16's primary sensor is the Northrop Grumman APG-83 AESA radar, also known as the Scalable Agile Beam Radar (SABR). This is defined as a multifunction, active electronically scanned array radar. It was developed as the replacement radar system for the legacy APG-68 type installed on countless USAF F-16sunder the Radar Modernization Programme (RMP). According to the US government's Director of Operational Test and Evaluation (DOT&E), the APG-83 provides F-16 pilots with air-to-air and air-to-ground situational awareness, high-resolution synthetic aperture radar mapping, fire control, and datalink support to air-to-air missiles. Airmen use the APG-83 with onboard weapons, to accomplish the full kill chain against air, ground and surface targets from beyond-visual-range and in all weather conditions.

Compared to the legacy APG-68 system, the APG-83 enables targeting and engagement from greater ranges, with enhanced accuracy and combat identification. According to Northrop Grumman the APG-83 can operate in dense electronic environments and can conduct simultaneous multi-mode operations. The radar unit is designed for installation as a form, fit and function modification that operates within the F-16's existing forward fuselage, with the original power and cooling capabilities, without making any major modifications to the jet.

Northrop Grumman developed a liquid cooling system for the APG-83 that is

Block 40 F-16D 89-169/ED assigned to the 416th FLTS in formation with the 412th Test wing's dedicated KC-135R tanker. USAF/Bryce Bennett

Block 70 F-16D 1611 loaded with an AAQ-33 sniper pod, AIM-9X Sidewinder, AIM-120 AMRAAMs and two versions of the Joint Direct Attack Munition. USAF/Richard Gonzales

ALQ-254 VIPER SHIELD ELECTRONIC WARFARE SYSTEM

The Block 70 F-16 is equipped with a new electronic warfare system called Viper Shield built by L3 Harris in partnership with the USAF and Lockheed Martin. This provides a virtual electronic shield around the aircraft, to protect the aircraft in complex battlespaces with improved probability of intercept against agile threats. The sensors that feed the system are embedded at locations around the fuselage to enable 360° spherical coverage. Use of an all-digital architecture enables a smaller form factor, reduced weight. and future upgrades.

Similarly, use of software-defined components enables a digital radar warning receiver (DRWR) and digital countermeasure capabilities in a fully integrated, internally mounted system, and a digital radio frequency memory (DRFM)-based jamming system helps to protect the aircraft from advanced threats. The DRWR is integrated with the system's jammers.

Viper Shield is designed to operate with the Northrop Grumman APG-83 AESA radar for RF compatibility, provides the pilot with a level of situational awareness greater than earlier Block F-16 aircraft, operates in active and passive mode and has a dedicated multifunction display. The system comprises fewer critical components than previous generation electronic warfare systems which results in a smaller form factor, reduced weight and a higher mean time between failure, along with lower lifecycle costs. Modular design allows maintainers to swap line replaceable units (LRUs) in the field.

Viper Shield completed its first flight in a single-seat Block 70 F-16 operated by the 412th Test Wing at Edwards Air Force Base, California. Major Anthony Pipe, a USAF F-16 experimental test pilot, said: "This flight launches the latest capability enhancement for the F-16 and our warfighters. The Viper Shield system combined with a Block 70 airframe creates a leap in capability compared to the traditional Block 50 Viper I grew up flying. The EW advancements this system brings will ensure pilots flying these aircraft continue to make it home."

The test flight included a series of risk reduction tests related to the mission computer and other avionics subsystem compatibility, as well as interoperability with the APG-83 active electronically scanned array (AESA) fire control radar.

Ed Zoiss, president of Space and Airborne Systems at L3Harris, commented: "Our building block approach to test hardware and software in labs, demonstrate functionality in dense radio frequency environments and validate the EW system on the ground prepared us for Viper Shield's successful first flight. Viper Shield is the only advanced EW solution that is funded and in active production for international F-16 partners."

Block 40 F-16D 89-169/ED is a long-term tenant with the 416th FLTS, which has operated the jet for 17 years. USAF/Bryce Bennett

completely self-contained in the radar. The coolant is chilled by an existing system on the aircraft, so no additional modifications are needed to fit an APG-83 to an F-16. This enabled Lockheed Martin to retain the same environmental cooling system used for the mechanically scanned radars fitted to earlier Block F-16 aircraft.

Implementation of the RMP seeks to extend the operational viability and reliability of the F-16 and provides pilots with increased bandwidth that allows the aircraft to detect, track and identify greater numbers of targets faster and at greater distances, to counter and defeat increasingly sophisticated threats.

The APG-83 can be used for the suppression or destruction of enemy air defences, including targeting radars and surface-to-air missiles.

AIRCRAFT RELIABILITY

In general, when new avionics and technology are installed on an aircraft, its reliability should increase. That's the case with the new F-16. One example given by Mike McSpadden is the AIFF CIT: "We went from four circuit card assemblies to one. Computation and processing are now done on a single circuit card assembly. Consequently, the aircraft's reliability is improved by eliminating the three otherd assemblies."

Other examples where components have been eliminated to increase aircraft reliability are a reduction in the number of circuit cards in the new flight control computer, incorporation of the advanced central air data computer in the new flight control computer and elimination of the aft crew station interface unit in two-seat F-16Ds. On new F-16Ds the aft crew station interface unit's processing is done by other computers with more processing power.

Increases in an aircraft's reliability increase its availability and reduces overall sustainability costs. F-16 maintenance includes time-interval phase inspections. Earlier Block F-16 aircraft have a phase inspection every 200 hours, whereas for the new F-16s the inspection interval is increased to 400 hours.

Explaining how some structural inspections have been eliminated based on the F-16's service life increase from 8,000 to 12,000 hours, Mike McSpadden said: "Some structural components are now inspected later in the aircraft's service life, so fewer inspections are required and the interval between inspections has increased, reducing the maintenance burden on the aircraft.

"The USAF took a very low-hour Block 50 F-16 out of service, which was used by Lockheed Martin for durability testing. The aircraft was placed in a full-scale durability test fixture and tested for more than 27,000 equivalent flight hours. We could have a certified service life based on half of that figure, so for the Block 70 we could have gone to 13,000 hours but opted for 12,000 as the certified service life for the Block 70."

According to a USAF press release issue on November 3, 2015: "The Block 50 F-16C was tested to 27,713 equivalent flight hours (EFH) during 32 rounds of comprehensive stress tests at Lockheed Martin's Full Scale Durability Test facility in Fort Worth, Texas. The airframe was then subjected to several maximum-load conditions to demonstrate that the airframe still had sufficient strength to operate within its full operational flight envelope."

Next, the aircraft entered the teardown inspection and fractography phase of the test programme. Test data collected over nearly two years was used to identify an extended, definitive flight hour limit for the airframe and demonstrate its safety and durability well beyond its original design service life. The durability test results were used to help design and verify Service Life Extension Programme (SLEP) structural modifications for post-Block 40 F-16s and to support F-16 service life certification to at least 12,000 EFH. The SLEP is designed to extend the service life of Block 40/42 and Block 50/52 aircraft.

McSpaddenexplained: "In the durability testing, we found 26 areas that needed improvement to get the 12,000 hours in addition to modifications completed by the USAF under its F-16 structural life extension programme. For the Block 70, instead of adding a stiffener or a doubler, or a structural component to deal with those areas, we built them into the bulkhead. For example, the aircraft needed a thicker web machined into the bulkhead. All 26 areas requiring modification were incorporated in the production."

Improving the structure of the aircraft is one engineering aspect, but what about the use of composite materials on the new F-16? Mike McSpadden confirmed that Lockheed Martin is working with the USAF on the development of a new composite horizontal stabiliser which weighs 60lb less than the original components: "That's of benefit given the growth in weight of the improved engines."